PRAISE FOR *DANCING ON HER GRAVE*

"Debora Flores-Narvaez, the Las Vegas showgirl, is front and center because Diana Montané always puts the victim first! The high-speed race-against-the-clock search for the truth of Debora's disappearance and the ultimate frustration in seeking justice is described in painstaking detail. Diana Montané and Carolina Sarassa push the envelope and treat us to another winning exposé."

—Mark Safarik, former FBI criminal profiler
and host of *Killer Instinct*

"Diana Montané and Carolina Sarassa have written a unique story about a Las Vegas showgirl's life and murder. I felt like I was there, playing blackjack on the Strip!"

—Fred Rosen, author of *Lobster Boy*

"A Las Vegas showgirl, a violent, heartless killer, and a meticulous police investigation, all set in Sin City and woven into an airtight tale . . . by Diana Montané, the grande dame of TC with numerous great titles in her bibliography, and cowriter and multi-Emmy winner Carolina Sarassa."

—Steve Jackson, *New York Times* bestselling author
of *Bogeyman*

"Diana Montané and Carolina Sarassa guide the reader through the sometimes-seedy underbelly of the Las Vegas Strip, a neon backdrop to the town where Debbie Flores-Narvaez met her demise. Montané and Sarassa provide a full account, behind the headlines, of the Flores-Narvaez murder mystery that caught the attention of the national media. *Dancing on Her Grave* is a story that needs to be told. It's the true tale of a showgirl who relocated to Sin City for a chance to break into show business but found herself hooked up with the wrong people. It's well worth the read for the historic perspective alone."

—Cathy Scott, true crime author
of *Murder in Beverly Hills* and *The Killing of Tupac Shakur*

DANCING
ON HER GRAVE

THE MURDER OF A LAS VEGAS SHOWGIRL

DIANA MONTANÉ
AND CAROLINA SARASSA

BERKLEY BOOKS, NEW YORK

THE BERKLEY PUBLISHING GROUP
Published by the Penguin Group
Penguin Group (USA) LLC
375 Hudson Street, New York, New York 10014

USA • Canada • UK • Ireland • Australia • New Zealand • India • South Africa • China

penguin.com

A Penguin Random House Company

DANCING ON HER GRAVE

A Berkley Book / published by arrangement with the authors

For information, address: The Berkley Publishing Group,
a division of Penguin Group (USA) LLC,
375 Hudson Street, New York, New York 10014.

ISBN: 978-0-425-28071-3

PUBLISHING HISTORY
Berkley premium edition / April 2015

PRINTED IN THE UNITED STATES OF AMERICA

10 9 8 7 6 5 4 3 2 1

Cover photo by Ryan McVay/Getty Images.
Cover design by Erin Bolles.
Interior text design by Kelly Lipovich.

FOREWORD

by Teresa Rodríguez, Emmy Award–winning
host of Univision's *Aquí y Ahora*

As an Emmy Award–winning journalist for more than thirty years with Univision, the Spanish-language television network, and its respected news magazine show, *Aquí y Ahora*, I've seen my share of horrific crimes and covered more than I'd like to remember. One assignment in particular became a ten-year labor of love and a bestselling book I cowrote with Diana Montané, *The Daughters of Juárez: A True Story of Serial Murder South of the Border*, in which I investigated and exposed how poor young women and girls in the Mexican border town of Juárez were being abducted and murdered, their bodies left to rot in the barren desert that surrounds the city. Despite the hundreds of cases that were never resolved or bodies that were never found, I remember the most difficult aspect of reporting these stories was talking to the families. I spoke to the mothers who kept their daughters' bedrooms as they'd left them when they disappeared, and who, years later, were still waiting for their daughters to return. Those assignments allowed me to report dozens of human rights violations including political and police corruption. Covering so many crimes in Mexico made me realize how little a life could be worth if one happened to be poor and a female. At this point, I thought there were few crimes that could leave me dumbfounded and shocked. That was until I saw Debora Flores-Narvaez's story. It was 2010 and the Christmas holidays were around the corner when this beautiful, educated young woman disappeared in Las Vegas. She was at the pinnacle of her career and moments away from starring in her dream role in a very popular show. Perhaps it was the time of year that her story made headlines, or perhaps it was the gruesome facts that emerged shortly thereafter, that haunted me.

Carolina Sarassa, the reporter who filed the story for our show, was no stranger to me. She was a talented, hardworking, inquisitive young woman who'd trained with us before she joined our Las Vegas affiliate. I remember the times she would come into my office and ask me about the stories we were working on and, in particular, about the art of interviewing and the importance of credibility and impartiality.

She was a woman on a mission, and I had no doubt

she was blossoming into an accomplished reporter. To see her investigation on the air made me proud, especially when I found out how persistent she had been in staying in touch with those connected to Debora's case.

I've always been one to believe that there are no coincidences in life, and when Diana Montané, the coauthor of my book, who also happened to be the cowriter of this book with Carolina, approached me to write the foreword, I knew that for some reason, I had to be a part, albeit small, of this story. Fate had once again knocked on my door to write about a Latina whose life ended all too soon and in the cruelest and most barbaric manner possible. This time, however, unlike the dozens of cases documented in my book, justice had been done; there was an accused murderer who would pay for his crime.

Carolina's dedication not only in pursuing this story until the perpetrator was brought to justice but also in making sure that it didn't just become another number in a growing log of cold cases was key. By securing interviews with Debora's family and close friends, she kept the case very much alive. It was her ability to develop a trust with those closest to Debora in life that would unveil the facts behind those closest to her in death.

Like any young woman pursuing her dream away from home, Debora's story of love and death could unfortunately happen to anyone's child. This was not a young lady whose parents were absent in her life; she wasn't a dropout, an alcoholic, a junkie, or a fanatic. She was a well-educated woman with a caring and nurturing family, and she had left the nest in order to succeed but inadvertently fell prey to a chain of events that no one ever suspected could end so tragically and morbidly.

PREFACE

by Roselyn Sanchez, actress and producer

The story of Debbie Flores-Narvaez needs to be told. It's very simple: no woman deserves to be killed the way she was. She was a young woman full of life, love, accomplishments, and health. Yes, she was an extremist; yes, she had a temper; yes, she got involved with the wrong person; yes, she was a Vegas showgirl. But she was also highly educated, a loving daughter, sister, and aunt, and all she wanted to do was dance.

Ever since I was a child I've noticed that nothing happens to me merely by coincidence or luck. I have always lived by the motto "My life is written." Countless times I have noticed, as a situation unfolds, that I was given a sign about it beforehand. It can be anything from a simple coincidence to a life-changing circumstance.

On April 29, 2014, I received a very interesting e-mail to my personal account from Diana Montané.

The content of the e-mail was intense, an overview of

a book she and her writing partner, MundoFox anchor Carolina Sarassa, were writing, titled *Dancing on Her Grave*. I read the e-mail many times, appreciating the kind words from Diana regarding my work as an actress and becoming rapidly obsessed with the case at hand. The case immediately grabbed me for many reasons. I love dancing, and in this case, just like me, the girl from the book was also Puerto Rican. I'm a girl with a dream of becoming a successful performer as well. I also left what I had in Puerto Rico to pursue a dream that my parents thought was out of reach. I also moved to a new city with great ambition to become somebody and be really good at my craft.

While I continue to work as an actress, which is my passion, I have wanted to find projects I could produce. I envision and pray every night for God to guide my steps both in my personal life as well as in my career. The possibility of helping to share Debbie Flores-Narvaez's tragic story with the world by bringing this outstanding woman's life to the screen and having the world see her kind soul truly melts my heart.

I believe one can have a connection with the souls of those who have passed away. I would love to think that Debbie chose me to represent her life. My immediate interest as soon as I read Diana's e-mail and the way everything is falling into place makes me believe I have Debbie's blessing to portray her life in a television movie.

I promise to take this responsibility seriously and give her the tribute she deserves.

I know in my heart I was meant to get close to Debbie. I also know for a fact my life story has one more dancing chapter. What a privilege to do it while somebody is guiding me from heaven.

Rest in peace once and for all, Debbie. Your killer was found guilty, justice has been served, and now the world will know and remember your name.

AUTHOR'S NOTE

by Diana Montané

Crime writers pursue stories as relentlessly as detectives pursue killers, and the chase is very similar.

It was sort of serendipitous, how I came across this story. Carolina Sarassa's and my investigation into Debora Flores-Narvaez's murder ran almost parallel to the real thing. She was then a reporter for the Univision Network in Las Vegas. I had previously worked with a young man, Diego Arias, at Telemundo in Miami. Diego shared on Facebook a story being covered by another colleague, Carolina Sarassa, about the search for a beautiful dancer in Las Vegas. Her name was Debora Flores-Narvaez, and she had gone missing on the evening an important rehearsal had been scheduled at the Luxor Hotel. Her sister, Celeste, had flown to Vegas from Atlanta in a fruitless effort to find her. It was a story that I, as a true crime writer and advocate for victims, could not resist.

I was instantly drawn to the story and messaged Diego:

"Would Carolina Sarassa be interested in writing a book with me about that case?" What were my chances of getting a reply? Diego was not a close friend; he was someone with whom I had worked. And here I was, messaging him out of left field, to relay a request to someone I didn't know.

I waited and waited, and supposed Carolina was either busy or simply not interested. But my fishing expedition paid off, and I reeled in my story, *our story*. Diego came back and said, very enthusiastically, that Carolina would love to.

Carolina was in Las Vegas, Nevada, and I reside in Daytona Beach, Florida, so Caro (as she is known to friends and colleagues) and I began to e-mail, and then talk on the phone. We felt like old friends and talked long into the night. I found her delightful, hardworking, and curious. We shared the same intensity and curiosity about cases; this would be a match made in crime-writing heaven. But frivolity aside, we both deeply cared about the victims in all of our cases. And there had been quite a few throughout the course of our careers.

In this instance, it all started out with the victim's sister, Celeste Flores-Narvaez, and her first visits to the station where Carolina worked. Caro described her anguish to me, and I, in turn, tried to capture it in words. We both really felt for her. Celeste had been relentless in the pursuit of an answer, anything that might lead to information on her little sister's whereabouts. So we both began talking with Celeste.

I had had experience in this area. The long, arduous road along the obstacle-ridden path of investigative reporting had been paved for me by firsthand experience. A nineteen-year-old college student from Miami named Shannon Melendi had vanished from the Atlanta softball field where she worked part-time as a scorekeeper on March 26, 1994. Shannon was an exemplary student, and had received a four-year grant to Emory University in Atlanta. I was then the entertainment editor for a weekly published by the Fort Lauderdale *Sun-Sentinel* and the *Chicago Tribune*, covering television among many other assignments. I was covering the television coverage of the Melendi case. *What a roundabout way of covering a case*, I thought, *covering the coverage!* So I decided to do my own coverage. I became friends with Shannon's desperate parents, Luis and Yvonne, and her beloved and lovable grandparents, Luis Sr. and Delia.

For fourteen anguished years, the Melendis did not know what had happened to their daughter, until the umpire at the softball country club confessed to kidnapping and murdering her on the very same day she'd vanished from the softball field. He had invited her out to lunch, and she felt comfortable with him because she knew him. They were in her car, and he then pulled out a knife and told her to drive to his house. There, he tied her up, raped her repeatedly, and finally strangled her.

Even after they were made privy to their daughter's premature and violent demise, I remained close friends with the Melendis; they lived quite near me. Yvonne, Shannon's mother, could be very funny, and sometimes she bravely tried to put on a face of normalcy. One night she called me up to ask if I wanted to come over. I did, and the two of us sat out by the swimming pool and had a glass of wine. Then we went inside, where Yvonne showed me a printer I was considering buying from them. She turned it on, and out came one of Shannon's college essays, one calling for stricter criminal laws, since she aspired to become an attorney and eventually hoped to sit on the Supreme Court. Yvonne began to read her daughter's essay out loud, sobbing softly and once in a while wailing, "Oh my baby girl, oh my baby girl." It was a guttural sound, from deep inside, and I didn't know what to say to her, so I just hugged her. And that was my first and not last encounter with a mother's, or a sister's, or a family member's grief.

Both Carolina and I felt anguish for Celeste Flores-Narvaez after she flew to Las Vegas from Atlanta to look for her little sister, just like the Melendis flew from Miami to Atlanta after Shannon was first reported missing. Carolina and I could not feel what Celeste felt, of course, but we had been through the process of interviewing bereaved families. I knew how Yvonne Melendi's body had felt, shaken and racked with unbearable grief, when I had hugged her that day.

Caro, too, had been through her share of heartaches and reporting at gruesome crime sites as a rookie reporter. She was a seasoned reporter and television anchor now, and she knew how to conduct an interview. For that matter, so did I, and so we set out together on the chase, to assemble the bits and pieces of Debora Flores-Narvaez's murder at the hands of her ex-boyfriend.

First came Celeste, of course, and her input was invaluable, but then we sorted through a long cast of characters of investigators, friends, and, eventually, prosecutors and defense attorneys. Some wanted to talk and were most helpful. A few were reticent and others were unwilling to talk, and yet we had to wait patiently for everyone to return our calls, to set a time to talk, and then write down what they told us.

Some people might think writing a true crime book is a much swifter and easier process than it is. We sort of churn it out in one sitting, they might believe, like they solve complex crimes within an hour television slot. But in fact this process took us three long years while the trial of Jason Griffith kept getting postponed time and time again, and during which a lot happened both in our personal and professional lives; and, of course, in everyone else's lives as well. Even Celeste had to move on, as she has two children to care for. And Jason Griffith languished in jail awaiting his day in court that never seemed to come.

As the case wore on for weeks, then months, then years, through a series of events I would hesitate to call mere coincidence, I was able to connect with the actress Roselyn Sanchez, who played Detective Elena Delgado on the TV show *Without a Trace*. A friend of mine told me that one of her daughters had been pals with Roselyn at university. Caro and I had always thought Roselyn—who bore a striking resemblance to Debbie—would be perfect to play the part if Debbie's story was ever made into a movie, but that was sort of a castle in the air idea. But after another friend and cowriter of mine, psychic Gale St. John, told me about this project that "there is a woman by the name of Rosalie or Rosalind, who is involved in it," I knew I had to pursue the actress. I tracked down Roselyn's personal e-mail address and wrote to her about Debbie's story. Roselyn—and her husband, Eric Winter—immediately connected with the story and came on board as producers.

Carolina calls Roselyn "our angel." I think she is Debbie's angel.

When the trial finally took place, it was all a matter of covering it every step of the way, and obtaining court records, as well as additional testimonies from people who testified. There were also the attorneys, and we interviewed both the prosecution and the defense. Fortunately, they were all very forthcoming, albeit sometimes hard to reach. This goes with the territory, and they were already busy with other cases.

So at the end of our thorough investigation, there only remained one thing, one question: Why? *Why* had Jason Griffith murdered and dismembered his beautiful ex-lover, Debora Flores-Narvaez?

I often wonder at some men's sense of entitlement that leads them to think of women as property, as something to do with, and then dispose of, as they wish. Fortunately, detectives and prosecutors feel the same sense of entitlement when such crimes become their own property.

Now that we are finally finished writing this book, we are hoping not only that it will honor Debbie Flores-Narvaez, and a promising life that ended all too soon, but that it will serve as a cautionary tale to other young women.

INTRODUCTION

◇◇◇

Debbie and Carolina: Parallels

Debora Flores-Narvaez was a thirty-one-year-old Hispanic woman who had moved to Las Vegas in search of a dream.

I, Carolina Sarassa, grew up in Miami, but I was born in Medellín, Colombia. My parents relocated to the United States so that we could live in peace, away from the war-torn city and the guerrillas threatening our family, and gave me the opportunity to pursue the career I have always wanted in journalism. Just like Debbie, my life has been full of dreams.

"If you want to make it in this career, you've got to move to a very small city." I can still hear the echo of Professor Dan Sneed's words during one of my Journalism classes at Florida International University (FIU) in Miami.

He was right, as I would find out.

When we first got to the United States from Colombia,

my parents decided to make Miami, Florida, our new home. It seemed like the perfect choice, since most people spoke Spanish and the Latino community is predominant. I guess it was easier to assimilate after such a drastic change. We'd had to escape Colombia with only a few hundred dollars in our pockets, but Miami welcomed us and became our home.

As an immigrant you always hear the cliché that "America is the land of opportunity." Well, the cliché was true for me; America has been the land of many opportunities, in fact. Still, while many people back in our countries might think, "You move to the U.S. and you can have it all," nothing comes for free. Yes, you can have it all and everything else you dream about, but only if you work hard, study hard, and do not forget to pay your taxes.

After graduating from high school, I was able to get scholarships from the *Miami Herald* newspaper, the FIU Honors College, and the Kiwanis Club of Little Havana to continue my higher education.

As I learned more and more about Debora's passion for school, it reminded me of my years in college. I am not embarrassed to admit that I was a nerd. I was a straight A student, always making it to the dean's list. Since English is not my first language, I still have a slight Colombian accent when I speak, and it was more pronounced in college. It used to embarrass me, but now I don't care. I actually think it makes me who I am.

I always knew I wanted to be a journalist. I enjoy reading, writing, and especially hearing and telling stories. When it finally came time to pick a major, I chose Mass Communications and Journalism with an emphasis in Print, meaning I wanted to become a writer for a newspaper or a magazine. I never imagined myself in front of a TV camera.

It was not until I met Professor Ana Ponte, a funny, smart, well-educated, and persuasive woman who convinced me to switch my emphasis to broadcasting, that I changed my mind. She also repeated similar words to those Professor Sneed had said: "You will need to move to a small market."

After knocking on many doors, and after completing internships, I was able to get a job as an associate producer for *Aquí y Ahora*, an investigative news magazine show based in Miami and the Spanish-language equivalent to *60 Minutes*. That's where I got to meet the talented, professional, and generous Teresa Rodríguez, one of the hosts (who also generously wrote the foreword for this book).

I worked behind the camera for about two years, then applied for a job in a smaller market, but within the company, in Corpus Christi, Texas. The news director,

Angel Covarrubias, believed in me, and he gave me a chance to fulfill my dreams. He guided me, and he also became one of my mentors.

So, that's how I ended up in Texas after living in Miami for eight years. Miami is a huge market for Spanish TV, but just as my professors had anticipated, the TV stations in Miami were not going to hire a young recent grad to be an on-air reporter. I had better luck in a smaller market.

Every time I had to move to a new city, it was difficult to leave friends, homes, and a whole life behind. But I had it very clear in my mind that I wanted to grow as a journalist, and that meant moving. That meant going to a bigger market. The bigger the city, the bigger the audience, and the bigger the market for TV. Many years had to pass for this to happen.

I still remember my first assignment as a local TV reporter in Corpus Christi.

A four-year-old child had fallen from the balcony of a fifth-floor apartment. His mother did not realize one of the bedroom's sliding doors to a balcony was semi-open. In a matter of seconds, so she said afterward, she realized her baby was no longer safe. When she couldn't find her son, she saw the door open. She was hoping she wouldn't see what she felt had happened: it was already too late.

The four-year-old boy was smashed against the concrete.

As a local TV reporter, the assignment desk is always

in contact with you and your photographer. Mary, our assignment desk editor at the time, called us and gave us some minor details of the 911 call she had heard through the station's scanner. She sent us to the apartment complex where the child had been found minutes earlier.

Corpus Christi is a small city, so we—the photographer and I—arrived pretty fast. I will never forget the face of the horrified mother, the neighbors, and especially the victim. His small body, covered in blood, was still on the ground.

I was only twenty years old. I'm a very sensitive woman, and back then, it was even more difficult to hold back the tears and hide my emotions.

It was a very poor neighborhood. The mother was in shock, while all of us had to try and do our jobs. We had to get videos and interviews and hope to obtain a statement from her; yes, from the mother who had just lost her child.

I remember telling my photographer how distressed I was by what I had just witnessed. It even made me question whether I really wanted to spend my career on horrible stories such as the ones I was covering every day. I went to the car, trying to hide from the rest of the media, and I cried. I finally was able to gain my composure and went back to the scene wearing my sunglasses, so no one could see how my mascara and makeup had smeared all over my face from the tears.

It all made sense a couple of days later when I realized there was a reason why I was sent there to cover that assignment. I had given my business card to one of the neighbors, and she called me. The mother of the child who'd died needed money to bury her son. We, and most of the other local media outlets, were able to do a story, and the woman received the funds she needed for the burial expenses.

I felt as if I somehow needed to be there, so I could help her.

Many journalists enter the industry for different reasons. I didn't look forward to becoming a war correspondent in the line of fire, or the reporter who broke the next political scandal. I wanted to help my community. I wanted to be the voice for the ones who cannot speak, or who are afraid to do so.

My next move would be to Las Vegas, Nevada.

After nearly three years in Corpus Christi, an opportunity opened up at a local TV station in Las Vegas. I could not resist it, so I did it again. I packed all my stuff and drove for nearly twenty-three hours to Sin City.

One of the things that soon struck me about Las Vegas was the high rate of domestic violence cases, especially murders. One would imagine most of the stories happen in or around "the Strip," the large street strewn with hotels and casinos, but this is not true. Most of the stories, at least the ones we covered, happened in residential areas.

I covered the most horrific stories in that city. I still remember Maria, a woman whose boyfriend threatened that he was going to come back with a machete to kill her if she called the police and accused him of domestic violence. She did . . . and he did.

Maria was walking out of her job at a gasoline station when the man, as he had promised, was waiting for her outside with a corroded machete. He cut her fingers and her hands and struck her many times on her head.

She was still alive when the paramedics arrived, and the boyfriend was still standing there looking at the pond of blood he had created. He was arrested on the spot, but although she fought valiantly, she never recovered from her injuries and died a few months later.

Maria was only one of the many gut-wrenching cases I got to cover in the city.

But despite sad stories like Maria's and Debbie's, I actually enjoyed my five years working in Nevada, and it was very gratifying to be recognized for my work during those years with three Emmy Awards.

My first Emmy was for best crime coverage, for a story I did about an undocumented mother whose husband had abused her, kidnapped their child, and took him to Mexico. Our efforts at the station were able to help this mother with a humanitarian visa, and her child was returned safely to the United States.

My second Emmy was for a story that really touched

some personal fibers. It was a series about the elderly who are abandoned by their loved ones at so-called homes. It was about people who are in the last stages of their lives and who rarely even get a phone call from a relative. Fortunately, in some of these places, the elderly are able to find a new family, sometimes even get married and begin a new phase of their lives. This series won the Best Historical/Cultural Program or Special.

My third Emmy was for a story I did about one of my passions: saving animals. When the Las Vegas economy started to fall, a lot of people simply abandoned their homes after losing them for a lack of payment. To this day, I cannot believe what these people were also doing—they would abandon their pets as well, simply leaving them inside their abandoned homes without food or water. Many animals died, and others were taken to local shelters where, sadly, due to overpopulation, many had to be euthanized. I tried to do my part, so I rescued four of them: Pippa, Coco, Mocha, and Marley (two cats, a pit bull, and a cocker spaniel, respectively). Mocha the pit bull recently ate all our sprinklers, but hey, she is a sweetheart; even the cats walk all over her!

The Las Vegas community is very welcoming to their news anchors and reporters. It's a community where people watch the news every day, and depend on us, and I think I was able to gain their trust. This was how I found out about Debora's disappearance—through a

Facebook message from one of her friends who apparently trusted me, too.

From the beginning, reporting on Debora's murder felt different. It did not feel like the other cases I had covered, and to this day I don't know why.

But I knew hers was a story that I had to tell.

ONE

◇◇◇

Showgirl, Interrupted

Her name was Debora. She was a showgirl.

When I first heard about the case of the missing Las Vegas dancer, the old Barry Manilow song from the seventies, "Copacabana," kept playing in my head. The tune tells the tale of Lola, a showgirl, whose lover, Tony, a bartender, is murdered by a gangster out of jealousy.

Would the story of Debora Flores-Narvaez's missing case turn out to be as ill-fated as the one in those lyrics? I wondered. After all, this was Sin City, and Debora's friend had sure sounded desperate.

Mia Guerrero, a friend of Debbie's, had reached out to me on Facebook. I had met the young dancer more than a year ago at a station event where she was modeling. Mia had come up to introduce herself and to tell me she was also from Colombia, like me. I was then the anchor for the Univision Network in Las Vegas. I covered the beat. I'd seen, and knew, the seedier side of the Strip.

Mia's message had arrived on December 16, 2010, at 8:59 P.M. She told me a friend of hers, another dancer by the name of Debbie Flores-Narvaez, had disappeared. Mia mentioned that her friends were also very worried about Debbie's whereabouts. She wanted my help as "a very special favor" to please try to air news about her disappearance in our newscast. Her message was kind, and ended with a "God bless you."

I was not going to sit on this story, and Mia did not have to wait long.

Debora had gone missing four days earlier, on December 12. It was sudden and unexpected, and, like most disappearances, her absence was what her family and friends referred to as oddly "out of character" for Debora Flores-Narvaez, whom everyone called Debbie. We began to cover her disappearance, even though the police were still treating it as a missing person's case.

Her name was Debora. She was a showgirl. But she also had a bachelor's degree in international business, a master's degree in international finance, and a degree in law. Her diplomas were hung proudly on one of the walls in her condo, in a building located across the street from the famed Luxor Hotel, the one with the Sphinx in front. It was called the Onyx Apartments.

But despite her academic degrees, Debora wanted to be a dancer. It was her passion. And she'd moved from Baltimore to Las Vegas in order to pursue that passion.

On the day just after her disappearance, her dream would've become a reality. Debora Flores-Narvaez had been only one day short of realizing her lifelong dream of becoming the lead dancer in a Las Vegas show, when she disappeared without a trace.

She had been slated to star as the lead in what was dubbed by the show's producers as "the Strip's most seductive, sensual show," the spectacle *FANTASY* at the Luxor. There had been two rehearsals scheduled on Sunday, December 12, 2010, one in the morning and one in the evening. Debora had attended the first one, in the morning, but she was surprisingly, conspicuously absent from the evening rehearsal.

According to authorities, the last person to have seen Debbie was her ex-boyfriend, Jason "Blu" Griffith, another dancer, who'd allegedly seen her for the last time on December 12 at approximately 7 P.M. It was Debbie's roommate, an aerialist named Sonya Sonnenberg, who had alerted the police to her roommate's absence from the *FANTASY* rehearsal. This was after another friend from out of town, Shannon Hammitt, had also phoned in her concerns to the police.

Investigators usually look closely at family and friends first when something like kidnapping or foul play is suspected. But Debora's case had not been ruled as either. She was just missing on a day when she surely ought to have been present, and eager, at her rehearsal. She was a dancer; this was her big break.

Her name was Debora, and it was Christmas.

As the days went on and there was still no word, Debbie's friends and family started to panic. Debbie's sister, Celeste, flew to Las Vegas on December 17, their mother's birthday, using up all of her savings, and borrowed a car to look for her sister herself. The city with its many lights seemed menacing, almost blinding her through her tears.

Celeste was a single mother, but she hadn't thought twice about leaving her children behind during Christmas. It was a time usually filled with toys, games, and merriment; a time when Aunt Debbie would have sent them presents and cards, and called to sing them Christmas carols over the phone, with her lovely singing voice. She was always singing, her friends remembered.

Family was everything to Celeste, as well as to Debbie, who had stayed in constant contact with her family until the night of December 12. Surely her tightly knit Puerto Rican family would have heard from her this month. Surely Debbie would have called on her mother's birthday. Debbie usually visited her family over the Thanksgiving and Christmas holidays—"She loved the holidays and would bring gifts, and we would celebrate together,"

Celeste said—but this year she had not been planning to go to Atlanta, where her parents and sister and nephews resided, nor visit any family in Puerto Rico, because she had rehearsals, very important rehearsals. But surely she would have been communicating in some way with her family, about her Vegas holiday plans, their upcoming family reunion, reminiscing about Christmases past. Celeste could not live without her little sister, she thought, and the possibility of losing her was becoming more oppressive by the day, as time went on and still there was nothing, not a word from the vivacious young woman.

Well, yes, there had been one text message Debbie wrote to her mother a couple of days before her disappearance, apparently in haste. It read: "In case there is ever an emergency with me, contact Blu Griffith in Vegas. My ex-boyfriend. Not my best friend."

Celeste had mixed feelings about the text message. "When my mom sent me the message and I read it, I took it to mean that if something happened to her, [Griffith] was the guilty party, but it seemed as though she was texting very quickly and left out some words. So, I then interpreted it as if something happens to her, to call him, he would know what was going on. I didn't think it was anything bad." Celeste thought Debbie might have been texting very quickly and had perhaps left something out. "It was like she didn't finish the text, you know?" she said.

Celeste added that when their mother asked if everything was okay, Debbie replied: "Yeah *Mami*, just keep it for your records."

At the time, her mother thought Debbie meant her ex could be helpful in case of an emergency.

The police refrained from comment. The PIO, or public information officer, Jacinto "Jay" Rivera stated during an interview with us: "We can speculate that she thought something was going to happen to her, but only Debora can solve this mystery, because she was the one who sent the text message. We don't know exactly what she was trying to communicate to her mother, or what made her send that sort of text message."

Las Vegas is a relatively small city with a population of just under six hundred thousand people. The dancer community is even smaller, and it's common for people to know one another, especially in the entertainment industry. Jason "Blu" Griffith and Debbie Flores-Narvaez had met in November 2009 at an after-party for "locals" at an indoor arena football, and they got together on Thanksgiving of 2009. Mia Guerrero, Debbie's friend who first reached out to me, was a fellow dancer, a model, and a very pretty girl in a city peopled with beautiful entertainers. She has long raven hair and a gorgeous body, like so many in the trade. She had met Debora at work, and they'd become fast friends. According to Mia, Debbie talked constantly about her boyfriend, Jason "Blu" Griffith.

"At first she talked a lot about him, always saying things like, 'I was with my boyfriend,' or talking about them being always together," Mia told me. "She always talked about how much she loved him, and 'my boyfriend this,' and 'my boyfriend that.'"

But recently, Mia said, she had also noticed that Debora seemed sad, that something was not quite right with her. "I not only noticed in her attitude, but in the way she carried herself. Even though Debbie was always a very private person, she seemed sad to me. Then I figured it had to be about her boyfriend, because she was always talking to him on the phone. I thought to myself, 'what is going on with Debbie?' She was always smiling and happy, always making everyone around her happy."

But there were obvious indications of trouble in the relationship. According to police reports, Jason "Blu" Griffith faced a December 2010 court appearance after a violent incident between the couple that had occurred that past October. The court report, dated October 21, 2010, stated that the defendant (Griffith) "did willfully, unlawfully, and feloniously, use physical force against Debbie Flores," by taking her iPhone, and that when Debbie went to retrieve it, Griffith had pulled her hair and kicked her. Apparently, he had also bashed Debbie's head against the windshield of her car.

As December 2010 went by and Debora was still missing, her smile seemed to be fading from her photographs we aired on television. Her sister, Celeste, appeared to be losing weight, and hope, very rapidly. On the nightly television news, she pleaded with whoever might have Debbie, "Let her go, and let her be, and let her come home with us."

And all I knew was that her name was Debora, and she was a showgirl.

TWO

<small>◇◇◇</small>

Sin City: For a Reason

I first visited Las Vegas as a tourist in November 2007, and did not particularly like the city. It was an enjoyable place for a vacation, but, as they say, I wouldn't want to live there. I recall asking the taxi driver what it was like to live in such an insane city as we navigated through the hustle and bustle of Las Vegas Boulevard. He got upset at my question and replied, annoyed, "You must know this is like any other city. I go to PTA meetings!"

In February 2008, I got an e-mail from a news director from Las Vegas whom I had met at Univision Miami. She told me about a weekend anchor position at her station. It was open—was I interested? Two weeks later, I was on a plane bound for the "insane city" to accept the offer.

While Miami, the seat of Univision headquarters, is nestled between balmy Caribbean and Atlantic waters, and its Latin population makes it warm and even boisterous at times, Vegas has its own peculiar sounds and sights. There was always something happening on the Strip, where everyone looks carefree and happy; oftentimes a bit too happy. The city might not be insane, but it is schizo-phrenic. For instance, there are the constant comings and goings of taxicabs carting off visitors, sometimes inebri-ated, to the casinos and the malls; the neon brightness that makes a stark contrast with the arid desert sands beyond its playful gaming enclave; and, of course, the police car and fire truck sirens that blare at any hour of the day or night.

Despite my initial negative impressions, however, I soon found that I enjoyed my work as a journalist in Las Vegas. After about a year anchoring on the weekends and reporting during the weekdays, I moved on to anchor the weekly nightly news. I covered various stories, from a strippers-on-wheels controversy—almost naked women who traveled by bus to different party destinations—to the high-profile O.J. Simpson robbery case at one of the casinos.

As a producer for one of the newscasts, I was always logging in to other media outlets to confirm that I hadn't missed anything for my show, such as any late-breaking story. It had been sometime past 7 P.M. on December 16 (shortly before receiving Mia's Facebook message) when I first logged in to the *Las Vegas Review-Journal* and read reporter Francis McCabe's article about how a showgirl from the show *FANTASY* was missing. Knowing it was the sort of story our viewers would be interested in, we immediately called the communications office at the Metropolitan Police Department and got a confirmation of the report. Minutes later, I received a media release announcing a press conference the next day. On December 16, 2010, we aired our first 11 P.M. newscast about the missing woman.

Just the day after Debora's disappearance was confirmed by the Las Vegas Police Department, her car was found. On the afternoon of Friday, December 17, Las Vegas police found Debora's 1997 maroon Chevrolet four-door Prizm. It was tucked away, in an apparent attempt to hide it, in an empty lot about sixteen miles from her ex-boyfriend Jason Griffith's house. It had no license plates, but the dancer's makeup bag had been left on the passenger's seat.

I went to the scene with my photographer to shoot some video of the area. The police had found the car through an anonymous tip, which later proved to have come from an area resident.

"The car was located in the northeast part of town, it was drivable, and a license plate was not attached on the vehicle," said Lieutenant Rob Lundquist of the Las

Vegas Metropolitan Police Department's Missing Persons Unit.

As I drove home late that night from the news station, I cast an occasional glance at my rearview mirror, the missing girl's image fresh in my mind as I passed the Luxor, on the Strip. I spotted the silhouettes of several young women walking alone and wondered, *where on earth could Debbie be?*

The dancer had last been seen leaving the Onyx Apartments, where she lived, near Tropicana Avenue and Las Vegas Boulevard.

Had Debbie been driving away? Had she sensed some imminent danger? Or had she run into serious trouble by some careless gamble, a stroke of bad luck?

My heart stopped for a second, and my reporter's instinct and my woman's intuition told me that something was very wrong. When I initially communicated with Debora's friend Mia, I asked her for a family member's contact information. She sent me the telephone number for Debbie's sister, Celeste, and later both women, Mia and Celeste, showed up at the station to be interviewed. At first, Celeste did not want to cry or accuse anyone in front of the cameras. But she looked like she was in a fog, and said the ordeal was a nightmare. Still, she tried to appear optimistic. "I'm not going to think I'm not going to find her. I'm going to bring her back with us," she assured us, and our viewers. Her outward confidence was not entirely convincing. Celeste and her younger sister, Debora, shared similar facial features, but Debbie's were softer. Both were shapely, pretty women with long dark hair and an exotic look, but Celeste was a great deal taller than her petite sister, who was only five feet three inches tall, tiny and compact, like the dancer she was.

Almost a week had passed since she vanished, and the search had intensified without yielding any results. Officer Jacinto Rivera, the public information officer for the Las Vegas Metropolitan Police Department, voiced the all-too-familiar ominous mantra: "The more time that goes by, the worse the outcome may be."

Despite the solemn news he delivered, Officer Rivera always tried to be pleasant, invariably polite, and extremely diplomatic. A tall, handsome man in his early forties, Rivera was born in Chicago, but his family was from Mexico, and he spoke Spanish with a Mexican accent. He became the spokesperson to all the Spanish-language media, and we interviewed him so many times a week at the station that people started asking him for autographs whenever he went out to a Latin restaurant with his family, or even to the supermarket. He was invariably amicable and often complied with these requests from his "fans," especially from the children.

All of the Las Vegas police officers, including Rivera, continued to work on Debora's missing case. During a press conference with the local media, the authorities said they had intensified their search for the missing woman, taking into account the possibility she may have left of her own accord. While certainly logical from law enforcement's point of view, that possibility always strikes a bitter note with family members and friends in missing persons' cases, especially if they feel strongly, as they did here, that that was not the case at all.

The invitation to that press conference at the police headquarters, located in downtown Las Vegas, read:

Metro Seeks the Public's Assistance in locating 31 year old Missing Person Debora Flores-Narvaez

Lieutenant Rob Lundquist, from the LVMPD Missing Persons Unit, took the podium and addressed the media on December 21, 2010.

"What we know is that on December 14 a missing person's report was filed by Debora's roommate [Sonya Sonnenberg], stating that she had not seen Debora for a couple of days." He then went on to say that the police had made contact with Debbie's family and friends, and had spoken with her ex-boyfriend. Though Jason Griffith was not named, Lundquist said of him that "he is cooperating with us. He did confirm he spoke with Debora on the evening of Sunday, December 12."

At the moment, Jason Griffith was only a person of interest, not a suspect in Debbie's disappearance. In any investigation involving missing persons, any person with knowledge of the missing individual is considered a person of interest to the police.

The Las Vegas Metropolitan Police Department has a great relationship with the community. Every time there is a case where they need cooperation from the residents, they call a press conference. The department is also very humble about recognizing the fact that many cases couldn't have been solved without the community's help. Their Crime Stoppers program is successful: it's one of the best in the country.

So, in the case of Debora's disappearance, they were asking for help.

"What we are asking the public, or urging the public, is that if anyone has any information, please contact the Police Department [through] Crime Stoppers."

The lieutenant did not leave out the fact that Debbie could have left on her own, though unsurprisingly, Celeste objected vehemently to the idea that her sister might have disappeared on purpose.

"She never missed a rehearsal!" she said, facing the camera. "It was the first day of rehearsal for her solo!" The past tense seemed to weigh heavily on her.

Celeste and I became instantly close, as if through some unspoken bond. In a matter of days, Celeste arrived at the station practically asleep on her feet. She told me that the past couple of days had been exhausting. Her nights became an endless nightmare, and the light in her eyes that was like her sister's sparkle seemed all but extinguished. She couldn't eat, sleep, or rest. She was on the phone constantly and asked me, every time she came, if she could leave some missing person's flyers with her sister's photo and information in the station's lobby. We always said yes to her, of course.

The mystery and the lack of information were very frustrating for local news teams—from every television station in Vegas, as well as print media—let alone for Debora's family. It was hard to maintain hope for a positive outcome. Celeste shared the same visceral feeling I had about her sister's car. "When they told me they found her car abandoned, my heart sank. I got very shaky and woozy, and felt really sick to my stomach, knowing the car was abandoned and my sister was still missing." She seemed visibly ill to me. It must have been unbearable for her to see her sister's face flashing on the television screen night after night, her life an open book of revealing photographs.

But again, on camera, the older sister gathered herself and appeared composed, hoping for a miracle.

"We want to bring her home to be with her family. We all love each other, and the family is not complete without her. We want her to come home!" she pleaded. Celeste was trying to keep her hopes up, and reassured us, and our viewing audience, and Debora's friends again, "I am certain that I will see her again, that she will be alive and well, that I will find her and everything will be okay."

On Friday, December 24, 2010—Christmas Eve—two hikers on the Arizona side of Lake Mead stumbled upon the charred remains of a woman's burned body on King-man Wash Road, about a mile from the O'Callaghan-Tillman Memorial Bridge, at around 11:30 A.M. National Park Service spokesman Kevin Turner reported the incident to the Las Vegas police. Although the body was technically found in Arizona, Las Vegas homicide detectives rushed to the scene, since sources familiar with the investigation stated that the victim had a similar body type to that of the missing dancer. By now, Debora Flores-Narvaez had been missing for twelve days, and this finding did not bode well.

Lake Mead is the largest reservoir in the United States, located on the Colorado River about half an hour away from the center of Las Vegas and the Strip. It is "the place to go" during the summer, offering kayaking and jet skiing, swimming, hiking, and wildlife viewing, although there is no dangerous wildlife in the area, only some tortoises.

But despite all the fun activities, the Lake Mead

National Recreation Area has a darker reputation as well. The lake is located at the junction of three desert ecosystems—the Mojave, the Great Basin, and the Sonoran deserts—all of which are known to be places where criminals try to hide bodies. Criminals in Nevada often hide bodies in abandoned areas of the desert or dump human remains in the reservoir. It is not uncommon to hear reports of a "body found" near Lake Mead.

Clark County, Nevada, coroner Mike Murphy advised that his office would autopsy the body immediately with the Mohave County, Arizona, medical examiner present at the procedure. Murphy gave no timeline for making identification, but said his office would work as fast as possible in order to be able to notify the victim's family. During the past couple of years, Clark County's coroner's office has had an agreement with the surrounding counties to perform many of their autopsies. They perform some from Nye and Mohave counties.

At Univision, we received a press release from the PIO's office asking us to please stop speculating. "It could confuse the family," it read.

Indeed, the very next day brought another wave of uncertainty to the investigation; after concluding the formal autopsy, the medical examiner determined that the body found in rural Arizona was *not* that of Debora Flores-Narvaez, the Las Vegas dancer who had disappeared almost two weeks prior, the coroner's office stated that Friday. The body belonged to a woman who owned an illegal brothel located in a residential area in Las Vegas. (While prostitution is legal in some nearby counties, like Nye County, where I once did a story about a brothel that hired the first male prostitute in Nevada, it is illegal in Clark County.) Apparently, two of the women's employees were later convicted of killing her. The motive: debt.

Almost two weeks had now passed since Debbie Flores had been reported missing after the thirty-one-year-old dancer had failed to show up for her evening rehearsal. There were national headlines about the case, along with renewed pleas by family as well as police, calling out to the community in hopes of finding the young woman. Tips were flooding in, but there were no viable leads.

By now, investigators had questioned several people and conducted a search of the home of Debbie's ex-boyfriend, fellow Vegas dancer Jason "Blu" Griffith. He was cooperating fully with police, but aside from Debbie's abandoned Chevrolet Prizm with its license plates removed and the grim discovery near Lake Mead that had turned out to be unrelated, there were no other leads in the case.

Griffith told detectives that Debbie had visited him at his home on the night she went missing. He added that they'd only had a brief conversation and that he had spoken to her through her car window and then she had left, and had seemed okay.

When Debbie first went missing, Celeste started to make the usual phone calls, to all of Debbie's friends. And invariably she would get the same empty reply: No, I haven't heard from her recently.

The older sister then got on her computer, thinking she needed to keep track of what everyone said, and keep a record of it.

She first phoned Debbie's ex-boyfriend, Jason Griffith, from her car, on January 5, 2011. And after the initial questions, she told him: "Look, Jason, I'm stuck in traffic right now. Do you mind if I call you in twenty minutes?"

Griffith was polite, but in retrospect it struck Celeste as strange how calm and nonchalant his demeanor was when everyone else around Debora seemed to be so alarmed. "I thought, after speaking with him as I got out of the car, something is not right here," she told me as she recalled this incident.

Through his attorney Patrick McDonald, who represented Griffith in the felony domestic violence charge from the incident that occurred that past October 21, 2010, Griffith volunteered for an interview with detectives, stating he was "very concerned about [Debora's] whereabouts and well-being." But Celeste was particularly taken aback by the discrepancies in the various accounts, not only of their relationship, but of her sister's last hours.

"Debbie's roommate told me, she left their house to go over to Jason's to watch *Dexter*," Celeste said, referring to the gory but popular TV series about the serial killer who hunts and kills other serial killers. It is a particularly bloody show. The rehearsal was late at night, so Debbie had some time in between. But Griffith had told her that Debbie "went over there, knocked on the door, and she was very calm, although they were broken up by then. He said that she just left, and he didn't know where she went." It was Griffith's characterization of her sister as "calm" that set off Celeste's warning signs. "They had broken up and she just left? No, no, no. I knew she wasn't going to just knock on the door and leave. She's trying to make sure she can get back with *you*. My sister is very strong-minded and very independent, but sometimes you think you can change a person into being a better person. As Puerto Rican women, we don't fail. We like to give a hundred percent. And sometimes, even though it's the men's fault, we try to blame ourselves. My sister, when she really cared about somebody, she fell head over heels. You really start to believe it, that it's your fault."

Celeste told us again about her first reactions upon

finding out her sister had gone missing, as well as what seemed a fruitless search for her, thus far.

"On Friday, I arrived in Las Vegas. It was December 17, my mom's birthday! I got to Vegas at 3 P.M. and the first thing I did was go to the detective's office. They weren't talking to me; they weren't telling me anything. Finally, they told me they didn't know anything, they hadn't found anything. When I asked them about her car they told me they found a little makeup bag inside it. But that's the only thing they told me. But then they did tell me they were going after the cell-phone records, the credit card trail, getting the prints on the car and the DNA. That's all."

On December 15, 2010, Detective Robert Garris had performed a records check on Jason Griffith, which revealed that he and Deborah Flores-Narvaez had a violent domestic relationship. Records showed three reports filed by the Las Vegas Metro Police Department. In one event, Griffith had been arrested for battery domestic violence and coercion, and in two events, Debora Flores-Narvaez was listed as the victim.

In the third event, however, Debbie was the suspect. On November 2, 2010, North Las Vegas Police Department patrol officers had responded to a domestic violence call at Griffith's address on Russian Olive Street. Debora Flores-Narvaez informed responding patrol officers that she and Griffith had gotten into a verbal argument. No report or charges were filed for this incident, for which she had been named suspect.

In the earlier incident where she was the victim, Debbie informed the patrol officers that on October 7, 2010, Griffith head butted her while she was sitting inside her vehicle. This head butt caused her to break the windshield lever located on the steering column.

Detectives viewed photographs taken by the crime scene analyst, which showed the broken windshield lever.

Debora Flores-Narvaez told the three officers who responded to her call that Griffith had assaulted her, both verbally and physically, when she went to the home of Agnes Roux, a dancer with *Zumanity* (one of the Cirque du Soleil shows) and Griffith's lover at the time.

The first responder to arrive on the scene after Debbie made the call was Officer Ryan Rowberry. What he found were two vehicles parked one behind the other.

According to the police report, Debbie had gone to visit Agnes and had then followed Jason Griffith in her vehicle when the incident occurred.

It wasn't noted if Agnes had invited Debbie over or if Debbie had gone to Agnes's house of her own accord, wanting to catch Griffith there.

The officers also could not ascertain whether Debbie had rear-ended Griffith's vehicle with her car, since there was no evidence of any dents.

During the October 21, 2010, incident, however,

Debora Flores-Narvaez told officers that she'd been inside her car when Griffith pulled open her driver's side door and forcibly took her iPhone from her. During that altercation, she said he'd hit her chin with his elbow, then walked away from the scene, holding her cell phone, and got in his car and drove away.

Debbie Flores-Narvaez and Agnes Roux both followed Jason Griffith, each in her own vehicle.

When Griffith stopped, Debbie stopped, and so did Agnes. And then an argument ensued between Jason and Debbie that became violent when he threw her phone about a hundred feet away.

According to Griffith's court testimony, he claimed not to have taken Debbie's phone until she began to follow him and threatened him with calling the cops.

Debbie had told officers she ran the hundred feet to pick up the phone after Griffith threw it violently, and then he caught up with her, pushed her down on the ground, kicked her, and pulled her by the hair.

When the officers arrested Griffith for domestic violence and coercion, they did notice that Debbie Flores-Narvaez had bruises on both of her legs, and that a piece of her hair was missing from her scalp.

It seemed as though Debbie had recorded some incriminating evidence against Griffith on her cell phone, and according to her, it appeared that he had deleted information from her cell phone. She definitely had threatened him with jail.

Jason Griffith appeared in court on December 22, 2010, to testify, but Debbie Flores-Narvaez did not, and could not appear to give her side of the story.

She had not been seen for ten days.

THREE

◇◇◇

The Headlines Turn Tragic

The news media descended on Las Vegas, the story making headlines at the local, national, and even international levels, especially given the glitz and glamour of the city. Also, and perhaps unfortunately, Debbie's own career as a dancer—sometimes topless—made the news of her mysterious disappearance fodder for more sensational and scathing venues.

Everyone seemed to be interested in the "missing dancer's case." Univision (both local and national), the *Las Vegas Review-Journal*, the *Las Vegas Sun*, ABC, CBS, FOX, and CNN were all following her disappearance, as were cable news impresarios like Nancy Grace and Jane Velez-Mitchell. *People* magazine focused on the text message Debora had sent her mother with the headline

"Showgirl Sent Ominous Message Before Disappearance," in their December 20, 2010, story. All of the networks saw it as a "sexy" story from Las Vegas. The term "sexy" is standard television jargon for a piece that has beauty, mystery, a love entanglement (preferably tumultuous), and yes, maybe murder. It was inevitable, if sadly ironic, that a story with all of the elements of Debora's disappearance would be labeled "sexy."

We at Univision were one of the first media outlets to start talking about the case, especially because the victim was a Hispanic woman and Univision is one of the main Spanish-language television venues in the United States (and in Mexico, Puerto Rico, and other Latin countries, as well as some countries in Europe). A producer from the Univision Network flew all the way from Miami to meet with us in Las Vegas. Typically, for a local newscast, the time allotted to each story is about one to two minutes maximum, since the newscast only lasts thirty minutes. But the international network show *Aquí y Ahora*, a *60 Minutes*–style news magazine program, wanted us to do a feature and cover the story in-depth, so my production crew and I made sure we had up-to-the-minute details. The stories for *Aquí y Ahora* last about nine minutes each, so they take a lot of preproduction.

We had all the elements in place, meaning the interviews we needed. (We had Celeste's interview, plus one from the police department's public information officer and another with a dancer who used to train Debbie. My producer, Wilma Román, a blond, green-eyed, and extremely professional woman, wanted to interview everyone who had ever met Debbie.) Our story was also featured on the international 5 P.M. program on Univision, *Primer Impacto*, another television news magazine format that also airs in-depth stories, and the first hard news of the day. *Primer Impacto* has the highest rating in its airtime, around 2.8 million viewers from coast to coast in the United States, and it dramatically increases throughout Latin America, Europe, and the Caribbean, which could bring it to 15 million viewers.

Per police reports, the timeline of events so far went as follows:

"On December 13 at 00.00 hours, Flores-Narvaez was a 'no call no show' for a scheduled rehearsal at the Luxor *FANTASY* show. Shannon Hammitt, an out of state friend of Debbie's, was the first person to report her missing. Hammitt learned that Flores-Narvaez did not show up for the rehearsal or the performance. Hammitt became very concerned and called the Las Vegas Metropolitan Police Department (LVMPD) to report Flores-Narvaez missing. Hammitt informed LVMPD dispatch that Flores-Narvaez was going to visit her ex-boyfriend, Jason Griffith, at his residence, on Russian Olive Street, North Las Vegas, Nevada. LVMPD patrol officers responded to the residence and made contact with Jason Griffith.

Griffith stated he last saw Flores-Narvaez on December 12 at 7 P.M. Griffith informed the patrol officers that Flores-Narvaez was fine and she had driven away from his residence in her maroon 1997 Chevrolet Prizm.

"On December 14, 2010, Sonya Sonnenberg, who was Flores-Narvaez's roommate, also called the LVMPD to report Flores-Narvaez and her vehicle missing. Sonnenberg stated that Flores-Narvaez was going over to watch the television show *Dexter* with her ex-boyfriend, Jason Griffith, at 8 P.M. December 12. Sonnenberg provided Jason's address.

"On December 15th, 2010, Detective Robert Garris went to Griffith's residence and came in contact with him in the driveway. He was in the process of changing the right tire of his vehicle, a 2005 black Chevrolet Cobalt, 2-door, bearing Nevada personalized plates. Griffith had a problem making eye contact with Detective Garris and kept complaining he was in a hurry and needed to get to work. Griffith stated he made contact with Flores-Narvaez on Sunday, December 12, in the evening hours, and he said she never exited her car. Griffith said he spoke with Flores-Narvaez through the driver's side window of her Chevrolet Prizm and she was alone in the car. Griffith described it as normal conversation and Flores-Narvaez left because she needed to go to rehearsal."

The day after Debbie's car was found abandoned on

December 17, 2010, the police department scheduled a press conference to make more formal statements about the case. They now confirmed that "foul play" was involved. The press room was full of reporters, cameras, and more questions than answers. Some people still thought Debbie might have disappeared on her own, maybe with an ex-boyfriend. That idea also crossed my mind, though Celeste's adamant refusal to believe it left me with doubts as well.

Now we were only lacking an interview with Mia Guerrero, Debbie's friend who had first reached out to me on Facebook, asking us to air a story about her missing friend.

I had called Mia on the phone several times, but since she worked nights as a dancer at the Tao Nightclub, one of the swankiest joints in Las Vegas, it was almost impossible to coordinate an interview until the weekend, when she'd have a couple of hours available in the afternoon. So on Saturday, January 8, 2011, we were on our way to Mia's house, all the way north of Las Vegas, when I decided to check with the police sergeant on call for the weekend to find out if there was any new information on Debbie's case.

There was.

Minutes after I paged the public information officer, I received a call from the sergeant. I explained to him that

I was working on a national story about Debora's disappearance, that I only had one more interview to do, and then I would start writing my script.

The sergeant told me that Jason "Blu" Griffith had been arrested the night before, on January 7, as he was leaving the Mirage Hotel and Casino, where he worked as a performer in the Cirque du Soleil extravaganza *LOVE*.

When I asked on what charges Griffith had been arrested, the sergeant replied, "Homicide."

He was very reluctant to give me any more information on the phone, but he answered my follow-up question, "So, if he's arrested facing homicide charges, does that mean we have a body?" in the affirmative. He told me, "If you need more details, come to our press conference at 3 P.M."

The second I hung up the phone, I called my producer, who had already arrived at Mia's house with the photographer. I asked her, "What do we do?" She spoke rapidly into the phone: "Just get here! We can break the news to her softly after the interview is over."

When I arrived, I found Mia accompanied by her Army vet husband and her seven-year-old son. Once I settled into their modest but beautifully decorated, cozy home, I faced one of the most uncomfortable situations of my career. Images of somber cops on television trying to break the devastating news to the families of the deceased flashed through my mind. A chasm was opening before me, separating me from Mia with my secret knowledge. I had to somehow fill the void with sound bites, force out empty words from behind my professional reporter's mask.

I began by asking her about Debora and their friendship, and we talked about how Debbie had once organized a party for Mia's birthday when her husband was away. But all the while what kept ringing in my head, like a death knell, was: *She is gone, she is gone, she is gone.*

The interview lasted about a half hour. When it was over, I told her, "Mia, I have bad news. I spoke to the police, and they arrested Jason." She looked at me with a quizzical yet knowing expression as I went on to say, "I assume Debbie is not with us anymore."

Mia was silent for a moment. "I . . . am . . . speechless," she finally said, pausing between each word. Then, through her sobs, came the words she had said to me before, as if trying to gather some lost pieces of her fellow dancer: "It's not the image I have of her, always smiling, always such a happy person!"

At the 3 P.M. press conference, our story changed in a matter of seconds. The case was no longer about the mystery of the missing Las Vegas dancer. It was about her murder.

The headlines turned tragic.

FOUR

◇◇◇

Cheerleader, College Graduate, Showgirl

After Debora's death, the mystery of her life only deepened.

She and her older sister, Celeste, were both born in Puerto Rico, though the family moved to Baltimore in 1987, when Debbie was seven years old. Thirteen years later, in 2000, when her parents decided to move to Atlanta searching for new opportunities, Celeste moved away as well, leaving Debbie, then twenty years old, by herself in Baltimore. Celeste recalled, "I moved to Puerto Rico for about a year and a half, but then I returned to Atlanta and loved it [so I] stayed." But Celeste wasn't worried about her sister, who was in college at the time, and besides, they had a lot of friends there, so technically she wasn't alone. Debbie's parents later divorced when she was twenty-three; it didn't affect her much, though, and she understood they had to go their separate ways.

More than anything, Celeste remembered what a good-hearted person her little sister was. She said Debbie couldn't stand seeing someone in need, and had to help them. "She was a generous girl," Celeste said.

Her older sister recalls Debbie as a well-liked "social butterfly" who made friends everywhere she went. In school, Debbie was a very popular girl, but that didn't stop her from getting good grades and wanting to succeed. Debbie attended the University of Baltimore, and then Towson University, also near Baltimore. She was a very dedicated and smart student. Celeste recalled, "She would just take more and more classes."

Debbie ultimately received three degrees, one in international business, one in law, and one in marketing.

But she loved to dance.

Since Debbie was a little girl, she'd had an amazing talent for dance, and she loved the attention she got for performing for her family. "Even though she was never professionally trained to dance, she took every opportunity in school, extracurricular activities and asked anyone who knew how to dance, especially salsa and merengue, the Dominican dance, to show her some new moves," her sister said. On our own newscast at Univision, Celeste reminisced in her English-accented Spanish about how her sister "was always practicing her dances. . . . She started to take dancing lessons and became a professional dancer. She was in ballroom and Latin dance classes, and I remember her telling me that one day she was going to move to Vegas. I was very surprised!"

But Vegas seemed an inevitable progression for the young woman who, according to her sister, Celeste, "loved the limelight." Before she was a professional dancer, Debbie had been a cheerleader at Old Mill High School in Millersville and then she'd successfully tried out for the Washington Redskins cheerleading squad, and there she was on camera, on a world stage.

"She was a good cheerleader in elementary and middle school and some high school," Celeste remembered. "She was always winning competitions. She did not go straight from high school to Redskins, though. She tried out for the team after she got her degrees." Debbie was with the Washington Redskins Cheerleaders in 2007 and 2008, a relatively easy commute for her, since Washington D.C. is only about a thirty-minute drive from Baltimore.

Being a cheerleader was glamorous work. (In fact, "Think glamorous!" their website encourages. "You may want to contact the hair salon for the Washington Redskins Cheerleaders to ask for advice on the perfect hairstyle for you." And they even list the website for the salon.) But also, according to their website, the squad "is more dance-oriented than cheerleading and stunting," and the dances emphasize jazz and hip-hop.

These dances were obviously right up Debbie's alley. She easily made the squad, and loved her stint there.

On her Facebook page, Debbie wrote the following poem on October 21, 2009. She titled it "JUST DO IT."

Too often we are scared.
Scared of what we might not be able to do.
Scared of what people might think if we tried.
We let our fears stand in the way of our hopes.
We say no when we want to say yes.
We sit quietly when we want to scream.
And we shout with the others,
When we should keep our mouths shut.
Why?
After all
We do only go around once.
There's really no time to be afraid.
So stop.
Try something you've never tried.
Risk it.
Enter a triathlon.
Write a letter to the editor.
Demand a raise.
Call winners at the toughest court.
Throw away your television.
Bicycle across the United States.
Try bobsledding.

Try anything.
Speak out against the designated hitter.
Travel to a country where you don't speak the
    language.
Patent something.
Call her.
You have nothing to lose
and everything
everything
everything to gain.
JUST DO IT.

Well, Debbie certainly didn't seem to be afraid. She just did it—right?

Cheerleading was not a full-time job, however. In fact, the Redskins Cheerleaders website lists having another full- or part-time job, attending school full-time, or having a family among their minimum requirements. After her tenure as a cheerleader for the NFL team, Debbie "started taking dance class, and became a pro," Celeste said. "She was in ballroom, Latin dance, you name it." The sisters never talked about work, Celeste said. "I was so busy with raising my first son," at the time (she later had another son as well), though she knew her sister was also working managing financial portfolios, and attending the university, first the University of Baltimore, and then nearby Towson University. According to her profile on

LinkedIn, a professional networking site, Debbie spent time as Senior Financial Analyst at Constellation Energy, Senior Manager of Financial Operations at Allegis Group, Financial Analyst II at Wells Fargo, and Junior Investment Analyst at Legg Mason.

In her post, she stated she had "roughly 9 years of Financial Analysis as well as Portfolio and Investment Analysis, Operations Management, Performance and Risk Analysis, and Business Strategy Management." She added that she had "excellent Public Relations experience," as well as a clear understanding of client relations. She stated she fully understood "the business cycle and flow of information, both financial and non-financial." And that she also fully understood, and had a strong grasp of, "both the financial and accounting principles as well as the capital markets." Her specialization was in multi-tasking with great efficiency and with strong interpersonal and communication skills. Flores-Narvaez considered that her success stemmed from her "ability to oversee multiple projects at once and build teams of 'Winners' to meet tight deadlines."

She placed special emphasis on her "organizational skills," which "enabled her to complete those projects efficiently and effectively." She also highlighted her capacity to learn "new areas of knowledge" in order to meet any expectations, no matter how high, of any organization.

The young executive had certainly been busy with her

financial career. It makes one wonder, why would a young professional woman exchange three-piece suits and heels for sequins and feathers? Why would she abandon a prestigious, lucrative career to dance on the stages of Las Vegas?

Perhaps because even though she had good friends, and she was working and being a cheerleader for the Washington Redskins, the wide world of sports was not enough. Debora sought a larger stage.

Tennille Ball, a friend of Debbie's who went to high school with her at Old Mill High School and later visited Debbie in Las Vegas in the summer of 2010, months before she went missing, also offered some insight.

Both young professional women had had lucrative jobs, but their hearts hadn't been in the nine-to-five upward mobility grind. Tennille had left her job as a manager at MCI (media control interface, the global communications group) to become independent as a holistic massage therapist and caterer for holistic foods, while Debbie left her position as a senior financial analyst to go into dancing. "We both loved dancing, but she took it much further," Tennille, an African American woman now in her thirties, remembered. "I did it for recreation and fun, but it was her life energy." Tennille added that the two friends would go out dancing with other friends about three nights a week. Debbie never talked about work. "We both kind of escaped from our daily lives by going dancing," Tennille said. "We would all go out to clubs, not only in Maryland but in Virginia. Some clubs have Latin Night, and whenever that was, there we were!" Her friend laughed. She also commented that Debbie was "exceptionally intelligent."

"If you have a passion for something, you can't fight it," clarified Debbie's high school friend. "And Debbie's not a behind-the-desk kind of girl."

Therefore, when her then-boyfriend Jamile McGee decided to move to Las Vegas in 2009, Debbie elected to go with him. The two of them had gone to high school together, and he was a dancer, too, and had been a finalist in the *So You Think You Can Dance* competition. So Debbie then fully committed herself to her dream, to dance.

Her big sister was not thrilled when Debbie called to give her the news that she was moving to Vegas. Their mother was particularly upset about it, Celeste said.

"I was so mad at Debbie," Celeste remembered. "I thought it was a terrible idea. She didn't know anyone in that city. At least in Baltimore she had friends. Las Vegas is such a crazy city and I don't know why, but I had a very bad feeling." She didn't want her little sister to move to such a crazy place. "In Sin City you get in trouble," Celeste concluded. Obviously, her little sister had.

Celeste added, "When she told me she was going to move to Las Vegas, I knew she was serious, but at first I was like, 'nah, she's going to change her mind.' But she did it. She left her studies and her degrees behind and realized her dream: dance."

Debbie lived in Las Vegas for two and a half years before she disappeared, and unfortunately, Celeste was never able to afford to visit until that December 2010. "Her life was radically different in Vegas," Celeste conceded. A sister knows. "She didn't have to tell us, we knew." She also knew without being told about Debbie's volatile relationships. "Well, when she loved, she loved all the way, no holds barred," Celeste said. "Of course, they fought; couples do not get perfectly along all of the time. She was a firecracker, very explosive at times. But she did it because she studied hard, played hard, and loved hard."

Debbie was apparently working hard, and loving hard, in Las Vegas. But Celeste did not know many details about who her love interests were after Debbie split from Jamile.

"I knew she was with somebody in Vegas, but I didn't know who he was," said her older sister. "I have children and I work during the day, and there are two hours difference between us," Celeste said, referring to the time difference between Las Vegas and Atlanta. "We'd talk about my kids and our family, and that was it. Sometimes I felt that she was sad and having problems, and I knew it was on account of some relationship, but I wasn't going to push her if she didn't want to talk."

It was only later, after Celeste arrived in Las Vegas to search for her missing sister, that she found out from Debbie's dancer friend, Mia Guerrero, that her sister had been dating another dancer: Jason "Blu" Griffith.

Mia described Griffith as "quite shy" and rather "non-descript." But Jason Griffith is a good-looking African American male, with strong facial features, intense, deep-set brown eyes, and a killer body, with defined muscles in his legs and arms, and the proverbial six-pack abs; he stands five feet nine inches tall and weighs a lean 165 pounds, which is all muscle. It is easy to see why women were attracted to him. Little did Celeste know just how much her little sister was attracted to the seemingly "non-descript," unassuming young dancer.

As close as the two sisters were, Celeste admitted that Debbie never confided in her about any problems the couple might've been having.

"My sister would just say, 'I'm sad today,' or 'We're not getting along today. My boyfriend and I are having problems.' Sometimes she would tell me she wanted to come home or visit, that she needed a break. But she never filled me in on the details. And she never came home."

When asked about her sister's previous boyfriend, Jamile McGee, the one Debbie initially followed to Vegas, Celeste didn't know much, either. She suggested that I try looking him up online, which I did, and I even reached out to him on Facebook, where he'd posted a spectacular picture of himself doing one of his flashy dance moves.

He responded to an interview request via a lengthy message on Facebook, in which he detailed Debora's behavior toward him and how it affected his life.

But after sending it, he asked that the message not be reproduced. He did not "feel comfortable" talking about his ex, he said, adding that it was a shame what happened to her. His Facebook page is no longer online.

Jamile McGee was also a professional dancer, mainly of hip-hop. He was featured in music videos and television reality shows. But according to a story published in the *Las Vegas Review-Journal* on December 23, 2010, Debora Flores-Narvaez filed a lawsuit against Jamile McGee, whom she accused of beating her, in August 2009. According to court documents, she alleged that she had suffered scarring as a result of a June 2009 assault by McGee in which she alleged that he'd kicked her stomach, dragged her from her car, and held her "hostage in his apartment while continuing to beat her."

In court papers, Jamile's attorney, Scott Holper, called the allegations frivolous and offered to settle for a dollar. But Debora continued her suit, and court records show that she ultimately won a $250,000 civil judgment. Damages were awarded to her because the scars cost her modeling jobs, leaving her with a lesser income of $40,000 per year from dancing part-time in a local show, according to court documents. Despite losing the lawsuit, Jamile McGee was never prosecuted by law enforcement; however, he had nevertheless left Las Vegas more than a year before Debbie's disappearance.

At the moment, investigators were not pursuing that angle, but I prompted Celeste for any more details about Debbie and Jamile's relationship.

Celeste did say that she knew Debbie had been in a relationship with Jamile for two years, until they broke up in 2009.

"Your sister never confided in you that there was violence in that relationship?"

"No, she never told me of any violence. But she would get very sad while she was with him. She would call me sometimes, crying. I was there to listen, like a sister."

I had to come right out with it. "Did Jamile hit Debbie?" I asked Celeste, but she didn't know anything more than what I did, which was that after Debbie had ended that relationship, she took him to court and was awarded a quarter of a million dollars for the physical damages he'd inflicted on her during one of their last fights.

Celeste interjected that her sister never did collect the money she'd won in that lawsuit; that it had been just a moral victory for her. But then she added something else:

"What I do know is that, four days before [Debbie] disappeared, she changed her mind, called her attorney, and told him she wanted to collect it. She called her attorney on December 8. She went missing on Sunday, December 12, 2010, and I found out about her disappearance the following Wednesday."

Matthew Guerrero (no relation to Mia) was another friend of Debbie's, and he recalled meeting the dancer shortly after she and Jamile broke up. "I met Debbie on a bad note," he said.

It was at Jamile's birthday party. Matthew, a dancer from San Francisco who had only recently moved to Vegas, was invited. Despite just starting out as a performer in a new city, Matthew's dancing skills were considerable, and he had quickly become friends with Jamile. At the party, in a reserved VIP area of the Drai's After Hours nightclub, Matthew saw a beautiful girl wearing a hat and camouflage pants come running toward their table all of a sudden looking very upset. She was obviously jealous and feisty, screaming because Jamile was there with his new girlfriend.

"Who is this girl?" asked Matthew, but he didn't get an answer. "Hey man, what the hell? I don't want to get into this, but what's going on, why is she so upset?" he remembers asking Jamile, who told him that the woman was his ex-girlfriend, Debora. Jamile went on to claim that she was stalking him, and now she was making a scene. After a long argument with Jamile, Debbie left, and the party continued.

A couple of days later, Debbie messaged Matthew through Facebook.

"She told me she wanted to come to my class, and I said, 'Yeah, sure, come to one of our rehearsals.'" Matthew taught a class at the Rock Center for Dance, a place very well known within the dancing community.

Debbie showed up to his class, and despite Matthew's less-than-stellar first impression of her, this time they hit it off while comparing their dancing skills. They even made plans to shoot a dance video together, which Debbie eventually choreographed. After talking to her for a little bit, Matthew said he turned around his opinion of her and instead thought, "What a nice and down-to-earth girl!"

They were both hungry after practice, so he invited Debbie to come along to his favorite pizza place in town, a small restaurant located in front of the University of Nevada, Las Vegas. He was impressed that Debbie, a girl who'd seemed to be so high maintenance, had no complaints and enjoyed her five-dollar pizza.

"I saw Debbie had two different sides," Matthew said. Everyone always seemed to notice the different sides to Debbie.

She spoke all night about her passion for dance and how she had moved to Vegas pursuing a dream, risking her career in Baltimore as a financial analyst by leaving it on hold. As Matthew later said, "Dancers, just like cheerleaders, are usually underpaid, [yet] they over-deliver because one of the needs they have is to be seen and recognized when they show their talents. It's their way of sharing their talent and connecting with others, which is a very primal need in human beings." As a fellow dancer, he understood that need and respected Debbie for it. "I enjoyed listening to her story. She worked very hard, and even though we had started on a bad note, she seemed very cool."

Matthew remembers Debbie as a good friend, a woman with a very big heart, and someone who would never take no for an answer. On their way out of the pizza place that very night, Matthew recalled a homeless man asking them for money. Instead, Debbie went running back inside, bought the guy a pizza, and gave it to him.

She helped Matthew with little things, too, like often letting him stay in her apartment when he was tired or had had a few drinks and didn't want to drive all the way home.

Although Matthew and Debbie became very close friends, the last time they'd seen each other was a little over a month before she disappeared, at a *FANTASY* show Halloween party. Matthew said that at the party Debbie had looked happy, she was glowing, and she was already excited about becoming the main star of her show.

"I was never friends with Blu," Matthew added, referring to Jason Griffith, Debbie's latest boyfriend. Even though the two men both worked on the same Beatles *LOVE* show at the Mirage Hotel and Casino, they'd hung out with different groups of people. Debbie's boyfriend's group had more seniority within the show. He was also the backup lead dancer for Sugar Plum Fairy, a part of the *LOVE* review, and did solos when the main performer was unavailable. Cirque du Soleil's *LOVE* is an interpretation of the Beatles' music (the title is taken from their song "All You Need is Love") combined with circus-based artistic and athletic performances onstage. Jason would often perform as the charming character Sugar Plum Fairy, who is completely in love with music and likes to dance. His fun character is a link between old-world blues and new wave pop.

But like so many people, it would turn out that Matthew didn't know all the different sides to Jason Griffith or Debora Flores-Narvaez, or even Jamile McGee, through whom he first met Debbie.

Jamile McGee certainly viewed her as someone with a difficult personality, and indicated that his attorney, Scott Holper, would be able to shed more light on this very gray area. When contacted, Holper did.

The Vegas attorney who had represented Jamile McGee against allegations of abuse at trial against Debora (who was in turn represented by attorney Luke Ciciliano) admitted that the lawsuit had been decided in her favor. "But I wouldn't say she won anything. She did not collect one penny from my client. My client did not have the financial resources to mount a vigorous defense." Holper added: "I do admit that her attorney G. Luke Ciciliano is a very formidable opponent. I think I would hire him if my wife went crazy."

Holper, in a roundabout way, seemed to be corroborating Jamile's statements in regards to Debora's mental instability. But then, he stated in a later verbal interview, "Debora was a beautiful woman who did not deserve what happened to her. I do feel that in some way her stalking behavior led to her demise. In some weird way, I think she would make up the abusive behavior in an effort to draw her mate closer to her, but this obviously did not work when her boyfriend was charged with domestic violence. To this day, I feel bad for grilling Debora on the stand, but her version of events did not make sense and I knew Mr. McGee was innocent."

It's true that Jamile McGee did not seem to fit the profile of an abuser. The biography on his website states that he started dancing at the age of four but was then diagnosed with systemic rheumatoid arthritis and told he would be in a wheelchair and not be able to walk ever again. Yet he presumably managed to beat the disease, and was not only able to walk again, but to dance on the world stage, giving his first professional performance at the age of fourteen.

Jamile and Debbie apparently knew each other from

high school, but he'd gone on to become a dance major at Wright State University in Ohio, excelling in ballet, modern dance, lyrical dance, and jazz, and performed at colleges and universities and special events throughout the country.

This all paints McGee as a dedicated, hardworking professional who had overcome the odds—not a violent man.

But things do happen behind closed doors. Still, I asked Celeste, why had her sister not told anybody in her family about her claims of domestic violence?

"Well, if someone beats you, you don't want to tell your parents; you think it's your fault. You feel ashamed, and you don't want to tell your family. So we didn't know anything about that. I don't know anyone who would want to tell her parents about something like that," Celeste said, though she added, "I never thought that would happen to Debora. She was a very strong person, very confident in herself, very independent. I never thought that would ever happen to my sister."

"I guess she was embarrassed to tell me," Celeste said. "She knew me. I would have gone there to take care of business." One wonders if she might have attempted to drag Debbie back home, although it seemed unlikely she'd have succeeded with her fiery and willful younger sister. Jamile McGee's guilt, however, was never established through the criminal system.

While attorney Scott Holper seemed to detect a logical progression, spiraling down from Jamile McGee's trial proceedings, Luke Ciciliano, the Vegas attorney who'd represented Debbie in her civil suit against Jamile, disagreed. Aside from being his client, Ciciliano, a man with a light complexion, curly, light brown hair, and blue eyes, said that the dancer "was like a little sister to me." He attested to Jamile's violent behavior toward his client.

"We presented evidence and photographs of her injuries. Violence against Debbie was very well documented. There were not only photographs, but home videos Debbie took with her iPhone. After we got a protective order against Mr. McGee, he violated it a couple of times. One time [he] even came to Debbie's and left her a card," Ciciliano said, noting that Jamile not only signed the card, "he dated it."

Ciciliano dismissed the allegations from Scott Holper that Debbie had been stalking his client.

"McGee was harassing Debbie, and as part of his harassment he filed for a P.O. [protective order] against her, which was thrown out in court, and at the hearing where Debbie was awarded her protective order, Scott tried to make the same kinds of arguments, that Debbie was stalking him. It didn't get him anywhere."

It was enough, however, to get the media talking.

Debbie's presumed stalking behavior was brought up and discussed on the program *Issues with Jane Velez-*

Mitchell aired on December 22, 2010, on CNN's HLN Network. Although Velez-Mitchell opened the discussion by stating she in no way wished to "cast any aspersions on the missing woman," noting that "she is the victim here," the host nonetheless mentioned that they'd gotten hold of court documents that indicated Debbie had previously been arrested for "disorderly conduct and accused of harassment. They report four people—*four people* [all of them ex-boyfriends]—sought protective orders against Debbie and three of them obtained those protective orders."

Velez-Mitchell then asked former sex crimes prosecutor Robin Sax about said protective orders, and Sax responded that while "disorderly conduct" was too vague to tell them much, protective orders do give a clue about someone's past history and motives, and that a restraining order against Debbie might have been evidence that she did have a "proclivity towards violence."

However, Sax added, it could also have shown who felt they had motive to "retaliate against her" on account of Debbie's prior behavior toward them. In short, Sax concluded, she might even be a victim. The protective orders, said the expert, provide "valuable clues to the investigation."

Ciciliano, however, was of the opinion that a lot of bogus protective orders come through the system. "So we might never know whether some of the allegations are valid." But, the attorney added, "The one thing I will say, knowing Debbie and representing her, is she kept her cool always. It took a lot to get her worked up. She was very levelheaded. She wouldn't have fed into it, is the point I am trying to make."

Jamile McGee's attorney also seemed to be concerned about Debora's well-being. "I wanted so bad to reach out to [Celeste] when she was in town looking for Debora," Scott Holper said. "Then, as soon as the news broke that Debora was missing, I told my wife, Margaret, 'She is not missing; she is dead.'"

FIVE

◇◇◇

The Music and the Mirror and
a Chance to Dance . . .

Debora Flores-Narvaez seemed so full of life, as evidenced by her photos and videos the media aired and kept almost obsessively reviewing.

On Google, the name Debbie Flores-Narvaez now brings up a ton of videos of news coverage of her disappearance, her murder, and the trial. But even before any of that started, Debbie was all over the Internet for her sexy, revealing modeling pictures. Her demo reel is still online under the name "Debbie's XO Modeling Reel." It shows professional pictures of Debora in a bathing suit, in lingerie, and in a beautiful red dress as well as some shots of her at the beach, all to the accompaniment of Fergie's pop hit "Glamorous."

And that was Debbie's life in Sin City—glamorous.

She was, after all, trying to make a living at her craft and move up in her career. It seemed immaterial, and par for the course, almost, that she also casually shed her top during some of the shows, revealing her shapely breasts. In that sense she was reminiscent of Bettie Page, the 1950s pinup girl notorious for her brazen disrobing in photographs and videos.

"The Strip's most seductive variety show," the billboard read for the spectacle at the Luxor Hotel that Debbie was meant to star in. "Women dancing around in close to nothing," noted in About.com teaser. And on the VegasLiveShow.tv website: "We actually had a woman take her top off in the audience!" gushed one of two dancers being interviewed. A former *Playboy* centerfold and *Baywatch* star, Angelica Bridges, performed in the ten-year anniversary of *FANTASY*, singing "Glory Box" and then singing and performing "These Boots Are Made for Walkin'."

Starring in *FANTASY* was Debora's ultimate goal, at least in Vegas.

Debbie was certainly ambitious, but she was also, like her friends described her, a down-to-earth, good-hearted woman. On her MySpace page she described herself as "well-cultured, quick witted, intelligent, considerate and humorous." But despite Debora Flores-Narvaez's advanced degrees, her accomplishments, her cheerleading feats, her dance training, and her spot as the lead dancer in a Vegas revue, there were certainly those who wondered if her "sexy" lifestyle contributed to what had happened to her. But that is like saying that she "asked for it," a cliché that makes victims' advocates see red. No one deserves to be abused, let alone murdered and discarded like so much trash. Debora was not "trash," nor is any victim, no matter what lifestyle choices or companions he or she keeps.

Of course, there are different types of dances and dancers. One cannot compare what happens in Vegas to the ballet, or to modern dance. There is an art to it, yes, but it is not the same. These dancers create characters, but in order to live out these fantasies with their bodies and to allow the audiences to fantasize about those male and female forms they see gyrating and contorting suggestively on the stage. And there is nothing wrong with the human form, when utilized consensually for artistic purposes. But surely there is a degree of exhibitionism involved in certain types of dances.

Debbie had been rehearsing for weeks with R & B star Sisqó, for a new number entirely conceived by her for the two of them to perform together as part of the *FANTASY* show.

Sisqó, whose real name is Mark Althavean Andrews, also hails from Baltimore, where the two had been friends. They had danced together in performances in Baltimore, and Debbie invited the singer to come and see *FANTASY.*

They planned to do a two-week run of Sisqó's hit "Thong Song," and it was Debbie's big chance to do a solo on the *FANTASY* stage. Granted, it was a solo with her friend Sisqó, but an opportunity to show off her skills on the stage without the rest of the dance corps.

"Thong Song" is indeed about that skimpy women's underwear garment, and knowing Debbie's style of dancing and the pervasive style of *FANTASY*, it was probably a highly suggestive dance. In the video of one of their rehearsals, she is showing Sisqó the moves, urging him playfully to slap his derriere. "Yeah, slap it!" she insists, smiling.

Kevin Peck, Sisqó's manager, who had the last footage of Debbie alive, gave the rehearsal tape to her sister, Celeste, as a memento. Kevin, who stated that he, too, had been a good friend of Debbie's, remembers the entire incident as "one of the darkest moments of our lives," referring to himself and Sisqó, who was not available for an interview. "He doesn't want to remember this at all," the manager explained.

But if *FANTASY* was the sexy Vegas show Debbie was meant to star in, there is also the one that can be found on YouTube, a video called "Sex Games," starring her and Jason Griffith.

"*Sex games . . . sex sex sex games . . .*" Griffith whispers on the video to rap music in a deep, throaty, and sensual voice. "*Will you play my, will you play my . . . will you play my sex games,*" and the rap beat turns insistent.

The "Sex Games" video might provide a piece of the puzzle as to the kind of relationship Debora had with Jason Griffith, and the way he viewed her. It is easy to stereotype, yes, but falling into the stereotype might have become all too easy for Debora when it came to men, and to the dance; almost like a parody of the brainy girl who described herself as having "a great sense of humor" on Debbie's MySpace page.

Black Latina writer Sofia Quintero offered her take, during another interview about the genre, on the sexism of hip-hop and rap:

> *Who holds it down at home for these men while they do their thing? Their mothers, grandmothers, sisters, home girls, girlfriends and wives, that's who. Who raises their children while they're in the studio or on tour? It's not their boys, that's for sure. But for all that unconditional love and support, a woman has no place in a rap song or video unless she's a mindless sex object or a ruthless femme fatale.*

Was Debora a "mindless sex object," which in turn caused her to act like a "ruthless femme fatale"? The "Sex Games" video with Jason Griffith certainly paints her that way: "*Will you be my slave . . .*" he asks, as she licks his chest, hungrily, and then bends down to bring her face up close to his crotch. Or is that too simplistic an explanation for a pattern of behavior that was growing increasingly more complex by the minute?

In spite of the steamy sexuality of the video, both participants seem very conscious of being onstage. There is no intimacy in the video; it's a game, a sex game. Debbie looks, sporadically, straight at the camera, suggestively and seductively. Griffith appears to be toying with his own reflection.

Dance studios are flanked by mirrors all around. Dancers are, by definition, body obsessed. "*All I ever needed was the music, and the mirror, and the chance to dance for you*," sings one of the dancers from the meta Broadway show about Broadway dancers, *A Chorus Line.* Which of these reflections was the real Debbie? Which one did she want people, and especially men, to see? Which reflection of herself did she see when she danced before the mirror, to the music? What on earth caused her to leave Baltimore, after obtaining three university degrees, managing financial portfolios, and earning a good salary, to enact these fantasies?

Once the dance in the "Sex Games" video is over, Debbie and Jason Griffith are seen playing a video game, taking turns at the joystick. That, too, seems like a reflection of the "*sex game, sex game, sex game.*" Griffith is excited and self-absorbed about the game, like a child. She wins, but he minimizes the importance of the win. And then they play again.

"I got you, I got you!" Debbie yells triumphantly, and then, while romping on the bed, she defies her partner, playfully and invitingly, "There is nothing you could possibly do right now. . . ." He interrupts her, jumping on top of her. She says something unintelligible about her neck. Then, his back to the audience, Griffith points to his rump, wearing briefs with the logo "Black Panther," slaps his behind, and boasts, "Yo, muddafuckahs . . . Black Panther's in da house."

Also on YouTube was Debbie's demo reel, where at one point she dances to the song "Down the Drain" by James Cappra Jr. Debbie recorded a music video for this song with her friend and fellow dancer Matthew Guerrero.

From the song:

I can hear the drip, drip, drip, drip, drop
is going down the drain, is going down the drain.

During the video choreographed and uploaded by Debbie, she dances to the lyrics, she and Matthew push each other, fight, cry, and then, just as in her real-life turbulent relationship with Jason Griffith, she goes back to him. She hugs him from behind, like begging him for love, for a second chance. More than a choreography, it seems like an act, like one of those dramatic Spanish soap operas. It ends with a close-up of their faces, Debbie looking down at Matthew. And apparently, "down the drain" is where Debora thought her relationship was going with Jason Griffith.

It is chilling to hear the song and the lyrics, and to see Debbie, so passionate about dancing, a woman with an amazing silhouette, so full of life on the screen. The video now, as of this writing, has over 31,000 views on YouTube.

I remembered what Debbie's friend Mia had told me about Debbie talking so incessantly about her boyfriend. "She always said, 'I was with my boyfriend,' or talking about them being always together." She always talked about how much she loved him, and my boyfriend this, and my boyfriend that."

The ABC affiliate in Las Vegas, KTNV, had published a statement online by Merriliz Monzon, another friend of Debbie's, on December 21, 2010. Merriliz said that she'd overheard Debbie on the phone with Jason Griffith on December 12, crying and pleading: "Just wait for me, wait for me, respect me, respect me, don't leave, don't leave!"

Merriliz explained, "It was obvious that it was her ex. It was obvious he wanted to resolve something via phone."

Merriliz, who had been expecting Debbie over at her house for Christmas that year, described her friend as "inspiring" and "powerful" but also told the station that she had witnessed "an emotional pull" that Debbie's ex-boyfriend had had over her.

"She's a strong woman and so dynamic and so lively. I felt like this was something she needed to vent from because she was keeping a lot in."

What was the fine line between reality and fantasy for Debbie? Did her exhibitionism border on obsession?

I was still curious to know what sort of relationship Debbie and Jason Griffith had really had. The *LOVE* dancer was known to date many women at the same time. Some of his friends called him a "womanizer," or a "player," a label that many guys do not mind. Griffith seemed to enjoy the attention, especially from the ladies.

One of those women was Agnes Roux, who was also involved in the assault incidents in October, when Jason Griffith had taken Debbie Flores-Narvaez's cell phone and then had allegedly assaulted Debbie.

Agnes Roux is a beautiful dancer for *Zumanity*, a resident cabaret show at the New York–New York Hotel. According to Wikipedia and the show's official website, it is the first "adult-themed" Cirque du Soleil show, billed as "the sensual side of Cirque du Soleil" or "another side of Cirque du Soleil." It is a show that explores human sexuality and describes itself as "a seductive twist on reality, making the provocative playful and the forbidden electrifying." The performers are truly risqué; some of the acts seem as explicit as the act of sex itself. The costumes are also in keeping with the show's sexuality. Most of them are minimal, colorful, and feature an extreme use of fur, feathers, lace, fishnet stockings, and cone bras to create a provocative appeal.

Jason Griffith was believed to have been carrying on sexual relationships with both Debora Flores-Narvaez and Agnes Roux at the same time, which is presumably why Debbie followed him to Agnes's home in October.

Both women had amazing figures, but they were very different in looks. Agnes has red hair and a very delicate face. She has a French background. Her name is pronounced with the "gn" the same way as "cognac," and the emphasis is on the "e" in Agnes, so that it sounds like Ahn-nyess. As a dancer, she has an amazing talent. Her demo reel is on YouTube, and one can only admire her moves as she delights her audience with her body. She has many different dance styles on the video, and her body is flexible and supple. She shakes her head, whipping around her long mane of hair.

Agnes was always competition for Debbie, who knew that Griffith had deep feelings for the *Zumanity* dancer. Agnes was also a highly trained dancer, while Debbie, who had no formal training and was basically self-taught except for classes she took here and there, must have had more than ample reason to be jealous of her.

But the redhead was not even Debbie's sole competition for Griffith's affection. Eventually, I sought out and met four of his other ex-partners. Most were fellow dancers, and maybe that made them attractive to him. Maybe he thought they were also on the same page about having an open relationship.

But one young woman, Marci Gee, was different. When she and Jason Griffith met through a dating site, Marci was working as a cashier at a cable company. She was a family girl, a very young woman from Guatemala—a *Chapina*, the term used for women born in that country. She was twenty-three years old, but she was naïve and trusting; at least, she was before she met Jason Griffith.

Marci has long, thick black hair. She wears almost no makeup, and her skin is flawless. She is a curvy, voluptuous woman. Her beauty is more innocent than most of the other women Jason Griffith dated. She wasn't a typical Las Vegas party girl.

Marci Gee was having problems with her then-boyfriend, so she decided to open a MocoSpace account (similar to MySpace, but more of a dating site). She was looking for a real relationship and not an affair. She did start chatting with other men, one of whom was Jason Griffith. He started the conversation, and she replied right away. His profile picture was very appealing to her, especially the six-pack abs revealed through his open shirt. As they continued to talk online, Marci told him about her problems with her current boyfriend, that she was having jealousy issues with him, which was why she decided to take a break. Then Marci changed her mind, decided to give her boyfriend another chance, closed her MocoSpace account, and did not hear from Jason Griffith for a while.

A year went by, and Marci's relationship with her boyfriend ended for good. The young woman was single again. She reactivated her account and was browsing for new friends, and there was Jason Griffith. Again. They chatted, but this time he wanted to meet in person. They arranged a meeting at the IHOP (a favorite location frequented by dancers after work, due to their late hours). The two talked for hours. He told her about his life, and she told him about hers.

The date ended at Griffith's house. He told her he wanted to show her the room where he recorded his music videos. It also happened to be his bedroom.

(At the time, Jason Griffith was living in a converted garage at his friend Louis Colombo's home. By the end of 2010, Griffith and Louis had moved out of that residence but were still roommates.)

Marci was impressed with Griffith's setup. The garage-room was very organized; it really looked like a recording studio. He had three Mac computers where he worked on music and videos. He told her he was on the verge of wrapping up a deal with Sony Music. That night, they had sex, and they continued to see each other for almost a year.

Marci said Griffith was always polite and a gentleman

and never seemed to lose his temper. He did not appear to be a jealous man at all. However, he did get rather upset one time, when Marci posted a status on her MocoSpace account that read, "I think I am allergic to condoms." He surprised her then by phoning her, very irate, asking her if she had had sex with another man. Nevertheless, after that incident, they continued to see each other, and as the relationship progressed, he opened up more about his life.

He told Marci that he had attended Juilliard, the very prestigious performing arts school in New York for dance, drama, and music, and that he had been able to fund his tuition with scholarships. (This was later corroborated during an interview with Gerald Gordon, his former acting coach in Las Vegas, who stated that Griffith had indeed graduated from Juilliard with a full scholarship.) Griffith then went on to perform as one of the backup dancers for the rapper Jay-Z, the music mogul also famous for being married to superstar Beyoncé Knowles.

Among the stories Griffith told Marci was one about his mother. While his mother was pregnant with his sister, he told her, the driver of a public transportation bus had accidentally closed the door on her belly. His mother sued the city and received a substantial sum of money. His parents were divorced, he said. His father was a professional photographer in New York City. He had apparently had an uneventful and even happy childhood and came from a middle-class family.

Jason Griffith himself had also been previously married, and he had two boys from that marriage. His dream was to become a famous performer. He and his wife and sons had moved from New York City to Reno when he got a job offer as a dancer in one of the casinos in northern Nevada. As he met the dance community there, friends advised him that he would have a better shot at breaking into the music industry in Vegas. He moved by himself and got a job as a backup dancer with singer Toni Braxton. Once he was established, he wanted to bring his family to Las Vegas. But, he told Marci, then he believed that his wife had been cheating on him. He said he felt betrayed. (This particular account was never corroborated. If his wife was unfaithful and had left the marriage, why, then, had he not gotten custody of the children? He did not clear up that matter, and Marci did not ask.)

He and his wife separated, and he stayed in Las Vegas alone while his wife moved with their children to California.

"He had tears in his eyes when he talked about his boys," Marci recalled, adding that Griffith told her his ex-wife would not allow him to see his children often.

As Marci continued to get to know Griffith, she met his roommate, Louis Colombo, and his friends, but she felt uncomfortable with the familiar way he treated his female friends. She objected to the way he behaved toward women in her presence, feeling that he was way too affectionate with them. They argued about it. She even told him, "I'm not a skinny woman and I cannot compete with your beautiful friends." He insisted that she was different, that he really liked her, and that the other women were just his friends.

It's not unusual for "civilians," as show-people and actors and other performers refer to regular folks with regular jobs, to have trouble understanding that it is perfectly normal for people "in the business" to regard one another as the closest members of their immediate family. It happens during Broadway shows, during television series and film shoots, and surely it happens with dancers. (It even happens among us newspeople, although we are never quite that chummy.)

But Marci was unconvinced. "He and his dancer friends were very close, almost unnaturally close," she observed. "I mean, they talked about each other's private parts, it was like they had all seen each other naked. I started to think I was the weird one!"

It got to a point when she could not take it anymore. She was having the same jealously issues she had with her previous boyfriend, so Marci decided to stop seeing Griffith. After they broke up, he would constantly call her and text her, asking her to at least be "friends with benefits," but she refused.

It was a few weeks after they'd stopped seeing each other that Marci ran a Google search on Jason Griffith's name and found the YouTube video "Sex Games," the one with Debbie kissing him all over his body. Marci phoned him and said, "Your new girlfriend is very pretty." Griffith replied that Debbie was just a friend, that he had "nothing to do with her."

But even though Marci considered Griffith "a player," she never thought he was a bad person, though he certainly had a few morally gray areas. He once told her, "I haven't been able to keep track of how many women I've slept with since I turned twenty." She also found out that he'd lied to her about his age. At the time they began dating, she was twenty-two and he told her he was twenty-six. "He listed different ages in his online accounts. Eventually I found out he was thirty-two." After learning about Debbie's disappearance and murder, Marci deleted photographs of Jason Griffith, and considers herself very fortunate.

Considering what happened to Debbie, she tells me, "I'm very thankful I ended my relationship with Jason. It could have been me."

It is painstaking, in more ways than one, to put together the pieces of this puzzle; not only of the disappearance and murder of Debbie Flores-Narvaez, but what, exactly, was her relationship with Jason Griffith? Between Marci's take on the man, and the stalking allegations about Debbie, her obsessive nature, and her own violent behavior, where was the truth?

Now that she's gone, her friends have made videos with her pictures, her own choreography. There is one post on YouTube that still reads "RIP Debbie. Beautiful Inside and Out." People knew her, she had friends, she had a family, and she mattered to many people.

Her name was Debora. She was a showgirl, she was a dancer, she was a person—but now came the news that she was also gone forever.

SIX

<><><>

Death of a Showgirl

Yes, Debbie was dead. And Jason Griffith, who had only been considered as a person of interest by investigators, had now been arrested and indicted on charges of homicide for the murder of his beautiful ex-lover.

Acting on a tip, investigators had found Debora Flores-Narvaez's remains on Friday, January 7, 2011, hidden inside the closet of an empty house in the center of the city of Las Vegas.

On Saturday, January 8, 2011, media outlets were going crazy. The big national story was the shooting that morning of Arizona congresswoman Gabrielle Giffords by a mentally ill gunman, who also shot nineteen other people, six of them fatally. But locally, all of the Las Vegas outlets were trying to find out what had happened to the beautiful burlesque dancer. A press release announcing a last-minute conference call went out on Saturday, titled "Metro Arrests Suspect In Missing Woman, Debora Flores-Narvaez Case." The press release read: "A suspect has been arrested in the case of the local missing woman, Debora Flores-Narvaez. Metro Officers will meet with the media this afternoon to discuss this arrest and other developments in the case."

Lieutenant Lew Roberts, Las Vegas Metro Police Department Homicide Section, was in charge of the conference. He is a very serious yet polite officer who was often willing to talk to the Spanish media whenever a Spanish public information officer was not available for comment on the scene of a homicide.

Most weekend crews showed up to hear what had happened. If you are a reporter and you are covering a crime, a last-minute press conference, one that cannot wait until Monday, is most likely delivering pretty bad news.

The lieutenant said, "Our victim was reported missing on Tuesday, December 14. From that point on, missing people began to conduct an investigation as a missing person's case. There came a point shortly thereafter that Missing Persons and the Homicide detail came together, began to look at the case, and conducted our investigation based on something we had found and tips that came in."

He went on to confirm the exact date that the victim had been reported missing and the fact that the police had already recovered her abandoned vehicle. He mentioned a tip that came in early the previous day, which led them to "a location in the downtown area where we were able to discover some human remains." He added, "As a result of that pretty reliable tip and the discovery, we were able to have enough probable cause to make an arrest on a Jason Omar Griffith, who was the ex-boyfriend of our victim. He is currently housed in the Clark County Detention Center, and our investigation is ongoing."

Griffith had been arrested early Saturday morning, January 8, 2011, as he left his job at the Mirage Hotel and Casino (where he was a performer; ironically, in the show *LOVE*), and he was due in court on Wednesday, January 11, 2011, exactly one month after Debora's disappearance.

The tragic end of dancer Debora Flores-Narvaez shook the city of Las Vegas with seismic proportions as an autopsy revealed her cause of death: she had been strangled and then dismembered.

The headlines now said it all, and everyone had the story, the complete story, about what happened to Debbie Flores, except this story did not end with her death, not by far.

People magazine featured, on the cover, "Coroner: Missing Las Vegas Showgirl Strangled."

From the *New York Daily News*: "Dismembered Body of Missing Las Vegas Showgirl, Debbie Flores."

Our own ABC affiliate, KTNV, announced: "Remains of Missing Dancer Found, Ex-boyfriend Arrested."

From CNN, viewers learned: "Dancer's Dismembered Body Found; Boyfriend Charged With Murder."

There were many others, including the obligatory segments on *Nancy Grace* and on *Issues with Jane Velez-Mitchell*, also on CNN.

But the succinct headline from TruTV rang truest in its finality: "Debora Flores-Narvaez: Death of a Showgirl."

Our story's TV headline read: *"Bailarina boricua fue encontrada en pedazos: Su novio la estranguló y luego la mutiló para esconder su cuerpo"* ("Puerto Rican dancer was found in pieces: Her boyfriend strangled her and then mutilated her to hide her body").

Although Jason Griffith's roommate, Louis Colombo, eventually made a deal with the police in exchange for a confession about what had happened, the first real break in the case had come from a witness who had a friend of a friend in the police department.

The police report states that on January 5, 2011, Detective Robert Garris received a phone call from Detective L. Cho, a female detective, reporting that a friend of hers had relayed some information from a witness named Kalae Casorso. Kalae, an attractive woman in her thirties, said that about a month earlier, her ex-boyfriend, Jason Griffith, had called her to ask if she would store something for him and his roommate in her apartment.

Griffith had met Kalae online, just like he met his ex-girlfriend Marci Gee. Kalae and Griffith met on a "hookup website." According to Griffith's defense attorney Abel Yáñez, the relationship was merely based on sex, but Kalae wanted something more serious than that. She was aware that he was dating Debbie, and would even offer him advice, although it got to the point where she thought Griffith was finally committed to her, but once again: he was two-timing her. They eventually stopped seeing each other when she found out Griffith continued to see Debbie even though they were trying to "make it work" as a couple.

On January 7, 2011, Detectives Daryl Raetz and Dean O'Kelley at the LVMPD Homicide Section obtained a recorded statement from Kalae Casorso during which she admitted that on December 14, 2010, Jason Griffith asked her if he could store some items at her apartment until he was ready to move. Kalae said she informed Griffith she didn't have much space, but that he could come over to see if the item would fit in a closet, or, if he didn't mind it being exposed to the weather, he could leave it out on her patio.

Later, she stated, Griffith arrived at her apartment and she showed him the space she had available either in the closet or on the patio. Kalae said she didn't realize that he'd actually brought the item with him, but he left the apartment to go get what he described as a plastic tub.

Some time went by, then Kalae said she heard cracking sounds outside her apartment, so she looked out the window to see a U-Haul truck parked outside with the back door open. She said she went outside, and as she was walking up to the truck, she heard a creaking sound from the back end of the truck, swaying from side to side. Kalae said she walked to the back of the truck where she saw Griffith and his roommate, Louis Colombo, standing on either side of a large, light blue plastic tub that appeared to be full of dark, charcoal-colored concrete that looked rocky on the surface. She described the sides of the tub as bulging out. She did not see a lid for the tub. The only other item Kalae said she saw in the truck was an orange dolly.

Kalae said she asked Griffith what was going on and what was in the tub. She described Griffith as hesitating, but then asking her if she really wanted him to tell her. Kalae said she told Griffith he'd better tell her if he intended to store whatever it was at her apartment. She described Griffith as hesitating again, then telling her, "Debbie is in there."

Kalae said that then she freaked out and told Griffith and Louis to leave and to get the tub and "the truck out of here!" The two men then left with the tub, Louis driving the U-Haul truck, and Griffith driving his black Chevrolet Cobalt.

Kalae said she hadn't called the police right away because, at first, she didn't want to believe it was true, and later, because she claimed she was afraid of Louis, a big man who worked as a bouncer at a club. However, she said she later decided to confide in a friend who knew someone at the police department so she could get help in figuring out what to do and how to handle the situation.

On January 5, 2011, detectives obtained surveillance footage and rental agreements indicating that Jason Griffith and Louis Colombo had indeed rented a truck and two utility dollies on December 14, 2010, from a U-Haul business located on W. Craig Road. When the truck was returned two days later, two males matching their descriptions were also seen dropping the keys in the drop box and leaving in what looked to be Griffith's black Chevrolet Cobalt.

On the evening of January 7, 2011, Detective Dean O'Kelley called Louis Colombo and solicited his cooperation in going to the Homicide office to answer additional questions related to the investigation into the disappearance of Debora Flores-Narvaez. Louis was still on the phone with Detective O'Kelley when he arrived at his residence, where Detective Dan Long was already waiting to offer Louis a ride to the police station.

Louis Colombo "agreed to tell detectives what happened if he would not be arrested or prosecuted on the condition he did not have anything to do with the murder," the report stated.

The roommates lived in a fairly new, two-story home in residential North Las Vegas, about fifteen miles away from the area where all the modern hotels and casinos are located. It was an unusual location for two relatively young, single men (Louis was separated from his wife) working in the entertainment industry to live—one would have expected them to either live near the Strip like Debora or in a swanky condo that said, "Hey, I'm cool and single." In Las Vegas, a twenty-five-minute drive to work is a lot, especially because everything is so close.

Louis worked as a bouncer (also known as a "V.I.P. host") at the club Revolution at the Mirage Hotel and Casino. Jason Griffith had gotten Louis the gig—the club was located in the same hotel as the Beatles *LOVE* show from Cirque du Soleil and decorated with a contemporary interpretation of the Beatles' era. Many of the performers are known to hang around at the lounge after the show.

According to the police report, Debora Flores-Narvaez had gone to Jason Griffith's house on the night she disappeared, December 12, 2010, supposedly to watch the show *Dexter*. She was last seen by her roomate, carrying a gym bag with her rehearsal clothes, since she was expected back at the Luxor Hotel that evening for practice of the *FANTASY* show.

It was Griffith's birthday weekend, and he had presumably asked Debbie to come over, but once she was there, inside Griffith's place, the two got into a fight.

The fight, as usual, escalated. Louis, his new girlfriend Maya Hines, and Louis's own children were present in the house during the argument and all heard the fighting, which at one point became so loud and heated that Louis had had to intervene, and even pulled Griffith off of Debbie because he was choking her with his hands around her neck. The roommate alleged that he told Griffith to stop, or he would end up harming Debora.

At that point, Louis said, he, his girlfriend, and his children all left the house, but he said that "when I came back, Debbie's [nearly] naked body was on the floor. He had killed her."

More than a month later, an autopsy would reveal that the cause of death had indeed been strangulation. And then the odyssey of concealing and disposing of Debora's body began.

We might never know if he premeditated Debbie's murder, but we do know he put a lot of thought into finding a way to hide her body. Griffith went to great lengths, and visited several locations, trying to erase all forensic evidence of the crime.

Griffith first took the dancer's car, after removing the vehicle's license plate, and abandoned it behind some houses approximately sixteen miles from where he lived. Griffith went to great lengths to conceal his beautiful ex-lover's corpse.

Louis went on to describe how Griffith purchased bags

of concrete at a nearby Home Depot, how the two of them mixed the concrete in their garage on Russian Olive Street, and how they filled a plastic tub with concrete to completely cover Debora's naked body. Louis said Griffith had cut her clothes off and taped her legs together in order to make her fit in the tub, face up with her knees to her chest. Louis said they left the tub in the garage to harden overnight until the next day, when they rented the U-Haul truck.

Louis said that they used the dolly to get the tub up the ramp and into the truck. After unsuccessfully trying to store the tub in an apartment in Henderson, at a friend's house, Louis drove the truck with Griffith following in his black Chevrolet Cobalt to the Flying J Truck Stop, where they parked the U-Haul overnight. (Louis would not identify the other friend of Griffith's in whose apartment they attempted to store the plastic tub.)

Then, Louis said, Griffith was able to get keys to a house that belonged to some friends of his who were out of the country for an extended period of time so they could store the tub there.

It later turned out that Agnes Roux, one of Jason Griffith's other lovers, was the one who'd been taking care of an abandoned home located in North Las Vegas. The house belonged to a couple, two performers, who had been deported back to Germany. Since the house was in foreclosure, she would go by once in a while to pick up the mail for her friends.

Griffith saw the perfect opportunity. Knowing that Agnes was planning a trip to Spain, he asked her to lend him the keys to that house. He offered to help with picking up the mail and maybe checking out the place, so he could possibly move in there with Louis Colombo. She trusted him and handed him the keys without knowing his real intentions.

Louis attempted to carry the tub inside the house by himself, but the tub started leaking. He then phoned Griffith and asked him to return with new plastic tubs, a sledgehammer, a handsaw, and some cleaning supplies. Griffith returned with the items, and Louis said that after he used the sledgehammer to break Debbie's body out of the concrete.

At this point, Griffith sawed off both of Debbie's legs with the handsaw, so she would fit into a smaller tub, then both men placed her torso and legs into two separate plastic tubs and covered her in concrete, stashing her in an almost reptilian way, like alligators hoard their catch underground, inside a swampy hole. Such a coldhearted, horrific act would be unfathomable to most people, let alone for Jason Griffith to do so to his own former lover. How could he not feel a thing after the sight of those dancer's legs?

Louis said they then filled each of the plastic tubs with enough concrete to cover her torso and legs and placed the lids on the containers. He said they put the tubs into a closet and sealed the doors shut with some kind of sealant. Louis said they also sealed the tools they used in a closet in another room so nobody would find them. He said they left the first blue plastic tub and the broken concrete in the living room.

Once the interview was over, Louis Colombo led detectives to the address where he said they'd taken Debora Flores-Narvaez's body. Judge Timothy Williams signed a search warrant for the residence, and detectives entered on January 7, 2011. Griffith had not yet been arrested. The broken blue plastic tub and the broken pieces of concrete were in the living room of the house, as described. A big piece of concrete left inside the blue plastic tub showed the clear impression of a hand, and there was also a large amount of long, dark-colored hair present. The front living room window was covered with a large sheet of black plastic. The window in the southeast bedroom was covered with a blanket and sealed around the frame with spray foam insulation. It had apparently been an attempt by Griffith and Louis to secure the home.

Later, in the early hours of January 8, 2011, detectives contacted Jason Griffith as he was leaving work at the Mirage Hotel and Casino. They asked him if he would be willing to go to the police station to answer some additional questions related to the disappearance of Debora Flores-Narvaez. Griffith was told he was not under arrest at that time, but he questioned the detectives as to why he was not being read his Miranda rights. Detective Dean O'Kelley told Griffith he would be happy to read him his Miranda rights before detectives asked him any questions. Griffith agreed to accompany detectives to the Homicide office, and while en route there, he called and left a message for his attorney, Jeff Banks, telling him he was not under arrest but that he was being asked to come to the police station to answer some more questions.

Prior to the start of the interview, Detective O'Kelley read him his Miranda rights, and Griffith initialed and signed the card indicating that he understood those rights. During the subsequent interview, Griffith was told that detectives had found Debbie's body, but he denied having anything to do with her death. He admitted to having rented the U-Haul truck but said that it had just been so that he could pick up a punching bag stand in the northwest part of the valley. When confronted about having driven to Henderson, Griffith claimed he'd gone to a friend's house to get more workout equipment, but he refused to identify the friend. He also claimed that he'd been in possession of the only set of the truck keys at all times, other than when his friend had driven the truck to pick up the punching bag stand.

When confronted with specific questions related to

Debora's death or the disposal of her body, which the investigators explained to him, Griffith told detectives he did not want to answer those particular questions without his attorney being present. Nevertheless, at the conclusion of the interview, Jason Griffith was arrested for the murder of Debora Flores-Narvaez. He was transported to the Clark County Detention Center to be booked and incarcerated. According to the arrest report, while en route to the detention center, Griffith told Detective Long that his ex-girlfriend had attacked him, and that he'd believed she had a gun inside her gym bag. He explained that what happened was not a "premeditated thing" and that it was "a heat of the moment thing that happened."

Was Griffith attempting to set up mitigating circumstances for the murder? Possibly. He probably anticipated a harsh sentence and wanted to cover all the bases. He had, after all, gone to great lengths to conceal his crime. And "premeditated" does carry the possibility of death or life in prison without parole.

Griffith told Detective Long that it was after the incident occurred that he did "all the amateurish stuff," later adding that Louis only became involved after Debbie was already dead, and that his roommate hadn't really known what was going on. When Detective Long offered to take a statement about the events of Debbie's death, however, Griffith still refused.

On Tuesday, January 11, 2011, Jason Omar Griffith

appeared in court for the first time. Due to the severity of the charges, his bail was denied.

Debbie's sister, Celeste Flores-Narvaez, also arrived at the court, visibly shaken and filled with anger, looking to face the man accused of brutally murdering and dismembering her younger sister. The encounter between Debbie's alleged killer and her sister almost became a scandal.

Celeste screamed at Griffith, "Look what you've done, you fucker!" and continued to shout expletives at him until she had to be removed from the courtroom by the bailiffs.

Afterward, outside the courtroom, she told the media: "I hope they do what they have to in order to send that devil straight to hell!"

Celeste said that at first she'd been infinitely sad, but now she was angry and demanded justice. On camera, she said about Griffith: "I want him to get the death penalty!"

SEVEN

◈◈◈

A City in Mourning

The first memorial service for Debora Flores-Narvaez was held at St. Viator Church in Las Vegas on January 13, 2011. A second one took place the next day, January 14, at the Luxor Hotel where the dancer had last been seen by some coworkers rehearsing for *FANTASY*. Her sister, Celeste, attended both, and was deeply touched by the offerings of flowers, as well as the various eulogies from Debbie's friends and colleagues, all praising her little sister's talent, her dedication, and, especially, her kindness to others. Before the body was transported to her native Puerto Rico, family and friends also held yet a third memorial, a vigil in honor of Debbie, a woman whose talent had lit up the stages of Las Vegas.

"Throughout the whole experience I felt just a sense

of the love that my sister had out there," Celeste later recalled. "And I completely understand what she loved about Vegas, and that it isn't just a party city. I felt complete support from the dancing and entertainment community. A lot of people think, oh 'Sin City,' they're party people. But they have lives and they work hard for what they do; it's their careers and what they're skilled at. I felt pure love. These people literally became a part of my family, even complete strangers."

Strangers were mostly who Celeste found at the church memorial, people who went to pay their respects to the beautiful, slain young woman; people who'd either seen her onstage or who'd followed the headlines and news reports of her initial disappearance, and then of her gruesome murder.

After the memorials, Debbie's friends and colleagues organized a benefit, held at the Crown Theatre and Nightclub at the Rio on January 26. The show was open to the public, and part of the proceeds were donated to Shade Tree women's shelter in Las Vegas, whose mission statement reads: "To provide safe shelter to homeless and abused women and children in crisis and to offer life-changing services promoting stability, dignity, and self-reliance." Other monies were used to help the Flores-Narvaez family transport Debbie's remains to her native Puerto Rico, where the family later held a private funeral in San Juan.

Celeste was unable to attend the benefit, since by then she'd had to return to Atlanta to her children. "But they sent me a video of it, and I cried all the way through it," she recalled, still tearing up. "All the dancers from the community participated. I love Vegas now! I was fortunate enough to see the best side of Vegas."

However, Celeste made certain her sister did not stay in Las Vegas.

"I took her home to Puerto Rico. I like to say I took her home in her brand-new shiny car," she said with a smile marred by the memories, referring to the coffin. Celeste described her sister Debbie's final resting place as overlooking a jungle, in a cemetery with "the most beautiful flowers, absolutely gorgeous; her place of rest is absolutely breathtaking." She went back to visit when she could. "I plan on going every year to talk to her, to make sure she's happy."

After Debbie's death, her older sister also had to deal with changes in their family dynamics. "My sister and my mother were best friends. I've always been the black sheep of the family," she said with a laugh. "But I was the strongest one, strong and opinionated. My sister was closer to my mom and dad. My way of showing love was different. She was more affectionate. Now my mom calls me every single day and I've had to learn to be more open with her. I didn't know how to be as affectionate with her as Debbie was. It's now easier for me to say 'I love you.' My father and I are pretty much the same, headstrong. His way of dealing with it is not showing his feelings. He is too proud."

Elsie Narvaez, their mother, a petite, soft-spoken woman with a kind demeanor and a sweet voice, corroborated this.

"Debora and I were very close," Celeste said in Spanish. "She was very warm and communicated with me always. When they were little, we were not rich or anything, but we had everything we needed, and played together with our dolls." She added that ever since Debbie was a child, she had always wanted to look her best. "She liked her little dresses. And then, when she grew up, even though she wasn't thinking of having children, she doted on Celeste's kids like a mother." Celeste's two boys, at the time of their aunt's death, were twelve and almost two years old respectively.

"My sister loved my older boy dearly!" Celeste said, recalling that the last call she had received from Debbie was to inquire what she should get her older nephew for Christmas. "The other day I was at a barbecue. As I looked at my son, I thought she will never see him grow up," she lamented.

Celeste wrote often, and sadly, about her sister on Facebook. Her posts are public, there for the world to see. April 29, 2011, seemed to mark quite an inauspicious occasion for her, as she posted:

I'm up watching the Royal Wedding countdown, the family and friends, the groom's men and the brides-maids, and all the dresses. It's a fantasy. Who wouldn't want to have a gorgeous wedding? I start to think about how mine will be, and then I realize that the one thing I'll never have is Debbie as my maid of honor. I wanted her to hold my bouquet and say that speech and toast on my behalf. It will never be a perfect wedding as I'd want it to be.

Everyone close to Debora Flores-Narvaez questioned why it happened, particularly why it happened the way it did, and whether there would be justice for their friend, their colleague, and, in Celeste's case, for her sister.

Debbie's former roommate, Sonya Sonnenberg, a beautiful and exotic-looking young woman who works as an aerialist—meaning she performs trapeze feats, on ropes, with scarves, while high up in the air—in Las Vegas shows, remembered that dancing was Debora's "dream job." Sonya was the person who called in the missing person's report about her roommate to the police. "She missed two rehearsals in a row for *FANTASY,* which wasn't like her, and we couldn't get ahold of her so we called the police.

"I met her when she started working at *FANTASY.* And I moved in with her about a year or so later," Sonya recalled. "I remember she was very passionate about life and about everything pretty much." Sonya said that as a roommate, Debbie didn't cook, but she was clean, and liked to decorate. "She decorated with colorful, nice things," she said. "And I remember her temper, too. She had one. She didn't do anything halfway." Although the two women were not "superclose," as Sonya put it, Debbie did confide in her roommate somewhat, and regarding Debbie's relationship with Jason Griffith, Sonya said, "I knew pretty much right away it wasn't a good thing."

As an accomplished aerialist whose work often takes her out of town, and even out of the country, Sonya had been away from Las Vegas and working in Arizona when investigators finally found Debbie and arrested Griffith. Sonya said she'd had a "bad feeling" when Debbie disappeared. Her reaction to her roommate's death was even more extreme.

"I was out town when they found her body," she said. "I got a phone call at five o'clock in the morning, from the police telling me she was dead. I collapsed. I actually fell on the ground and started crying, 'that is a terrible, terrible thing.'" The aerialist noted that she'd been half expecting an outcome like this. "By then she had been missing for a month, so I was waiting for that phone call." But if the phone call itself did not take Sonya by surprise, the circumstances did. "I didn't expect we would find her alive, but I didn't think he would go to those lengths,"

she said, referring to the dismemberment and concealment of the body.

Another of Debbie's colleagues was Rene Delgadillo,
who offered a fuller, and more violent, account both of
the relationship and of what might have happened to
Debbie. Rene, a choreographer and magician, fits the
image of an old-fashioned magician, with his slicked-back
black hair and moustache and catlike moves. Debbie had
been one of the partners in his "Salsa Magic" act (which
involved Latin dance), and the two of them had worked
hard together, he said. They'd known each other for almost two years.

"She was having some issues with her previous boyfriend. She said he had beaten her up," Rene said, referring to Jamile McGee. But recently, the dancer had been
calling up her magician friend, Rene, about yet another
relationship gone wrong.

"She was calling me crying and depressed, and I would
ask what was wrong. Blu was cheating on her"—Rene
referred to Griffith by his stage name—"and it was almost
like a love triangle. And she would say, 'I don't care if he's
with another girl as long as he's with me.' I would tell
her, 'Debbie you need to get out of this thing before
something happens.' I saw the red flags. I knew something was coming, [but] I was in shock when that happened. I knew something would happen but not to that

degree. I was totally blown away. She was really secretive about it."

Rene recalled one particular incident that attested to the violence in the relationship. The magician didn't seem all too fond of his close friend's then-boyfriend.

"One time, she came over to my house, and her car was all bashed up, the turn signals were broken, and she said she got in an accident. But things were broken inside the car, and then when I read the report, I saw that Blu had smashed her face against the windshield and that she broke some of her teeth inside her car. It didn't add up. She didn't seem to want to let go, but she was getting abused."

Tennille Ball, Debbie's high school friend from Baltimore, also had a sinister take on the entire incident.

"She was in love with Blu," Tennille said about Debbie's relationship with Jason Griffith. "And the way that he killed her was out of a horror movie. He just went too far. I don't think anybody who is normal does anything like that. We all go through relationships like that, where we argue back and forth, but what he did was beyond belief. He's a sociopath! And I believe he preyed on the fact that she loved him to lure her over there because he wanted to hurt her. It was his birthday weekend. He invited her over to watch *Dexter*, which was his favorite show? A guy who kills people and ties them up with saran wrap? Come on!" Tennille laughed sarcastically. And then she added, "I come from a police family and I know how to look for clues. And when I started investigating it was all there, in black and white. She was going to testify against him in court after he assaulted her in October, so he thought he would just get rid of her."

Both Rene Delgadillo and Sonya Sonnenberg went to the church memorial to pay their respects to their friend, as well as to the memorial at the Luxor Hotel. Tennille Ball, who lived across the country, could not, but she remembers her friend fondly. "I remember how much fun and how passionate she was," she said.

"Fun" was the word Rene Delgadillo used to describe Debbie as well. "What I remember about her the most," he said, "is how silly and how much fun she could be. She was a little feisty at times, but we laughed a lot. She was cheerful and extremely responsible, willing to give a hand to anyone. She was very kind."

Even Debbie's former lawyer, Luke Ciciliano, offered his view, as both a friend and an attorney.

"Debbie is someone who is full of life," he stated, using the present tense. "I have a framed photo of her in my house and it says 'Live, Laugh, Love.' She was full of passion; she just loved experiencing things. She always saw the best in everybody, and she had such a passion for the dance I can understand why she was attracted to other dancers. She could sit around her apartment all day and watch dance videos."

I soon learned that Debbie's innate kindness and friendliness extended beyond her professional circle, as well.

About two years before I began to cover Debora Flores-Narvaez's missing person's case, I went to grab a late-night snack at a Denny's with a colleague after our telecast. Denny's is, of course, open all night, so like IHOP, it's a popular establishment among those who work all hours. Our server at Denny's was a nice man named Lorenzo Buitrón, the type of server who engages clients in easy, polite conversation and is helpful yet unobtrusive. He even gave us his telephone number, since both my colleague and I were relatively new in town, telling us he knew lots of people.

As it turned out, one of those people he knew was Debora Flores-Narvaez. When Debbie was first reported missing, he called the newsroom to ask us for more information about her disappearance. Later, as I went through a mental list of other people who might have been casual observers to Debbie and Jason Griffith's turbulent relationship, Lorenzo came to mind, and I called him.

He knew even more about Debbie than I'd thought. Apparently, ever since she'd moved to Las Vegas and started working as a showgirl, she ate regularly at that Denny's on Las Vegas Boulevard, just a few blocks away from the Luxor Hotel. (She always ordered the kids' meal.)

About a year before she went missing, Debbie had begun to frequent the family restaurant with Jason Griffith, whom she referred as "my boyfriend." "She was all over him," Lorenzo remembers. They always requested a table in the back of the restaurant, away from the rest of the late-night crowd. She was always friendly and open with the server, whereas her companion hardly looked at him. Debbie would invariably pick up the tab.

Lorenzo describes Debbie as a beautiful, fun, and outgoing woman. One day he even asked her "why such a pretty girl was going out with such an ugly man." Jason Griffith was deemed as "hot" by other women, but to Lorenzo Buitrón, Griffith did not seem an adequate counterpart for beautiful Debbie. "I was just joking with her. She just laughed it off," he said. At that point, Lorenzo had felt comfortable enough with his regular customer to joke around with her like that.

Griffith wasn't the only man Debbie would show up with at his restaurant, however. She also kissed and was affectionate with other men, he remembers. But he didn't care one way or the other—Debbie was his friend, not Griffith. Lorenzo even went to see Debbie perform at the Luxor when she gave him comp tickets. The server, who didn't have the money to pay the pricey admission fees to see a Las Vegas revue, was thankful for the gesture and thoroughly enjoyed the spectacles. And he knew that she had been practicing many hours a day because of her solo role in the next Las Vegas extravaganza at the hotel where she worked.

But a couple of weeks before Debbie's demise, Lorenzo said, she changed. She became quiet, not at all talkative, seemed even frightened, and often cried. She continued to order her usual, but often she did not even taste the meal.

On the Thursday before Debbie disappeared, December 9, 2010, Lorenzo recalled that the couple showed up at the restaurant at around 11 P.M. Through the window, Lorenzo noticed them arrive in separate cars. The dancer told the server she wanted a table in a private area, even though at that time of night, that area of the restaurant remains closed and tables are not available. "I came to break up with him," she told her friend. At this point, Debbie probably knew that Jason Griffith was still having an affair with *Zumanity* dancer Agnes Roux.

This didn't surprise him, although Lorenzo characterized Debbie's relationship with Jason Griffith as "very confusing." He said, "One day, they were a couple and seemed all happy and all over each other; the next day, she wouldn't want me to even ask how he was doing."

Lorenzo sat them in the private area, but his manager was there, so he could not pay much attention to their table. But he did see the couple arguing, and noticed Debbie was crying. About an hour later, two other men walked over to the couple, and the four of them started talking. Debbie left a couple of minutes later, by herself. It was curious, in light of Griffith's allegations afterward, that Debbie did not argue with him or follow him that night. Lorenzo was used to seeing them argue often.

That was the last time Lorenzo Buitrón saw Debbie alive. It was a few days later that he was at a Starbucks when he opened up a newspaper to read his friend was missing. He said he was stunned, just like everyone else was, when they found out what happened to her.

EIGHT

◇◇◇

Dancer in the Dark

It was now spring of 2011, and several months had passed since we'd stopped covering Debora Flores-Narvaez's murder case on a daily basis. Time went on and new stories developed and became the new headlines.

As a reporter for a local TV station, I covered many cases. Every one of them is important, of course, but unfortunately, or perhaps fortunately, unless someone asks or reminds me about a particular case, I usually don't think about it. I don't take work home with me. But Debora Flores-Narvaez's murder was different. I thought about it every day. Early in the case, I remember going to a farewell party for a Colombian friend, Maria Fernanda, at a local casino in Las Vegas. That night, the nightclub was full. On several occasions, I thought I spotted Debbie among the crowd. Of course it wasn't her, but I had been talking about her for days now, which is something I don't normally do.

My husband, Andrés, would patiently listen to my endless stories about the missing dancer. Even my mother, Leticia, would ask me about her, and she cried thinking about Debbie's mom when I told her that the dancer had been found dead.

On one occasion, when the mystery of what had happened to Debbie had deepened and was still unsolved, as I was driving back home from the office at almost midnight, I began thinking of her. *Was she alive? Had she run away? Was her dead body lying somewhere in the desert? Had she met a rich and handsome man and run away with him to an exotic island?* Silly musings straight out of one of those lavish Mexican soap operas, the telenovelas that aired on our parent network, Univision. But as all those thoughts crossed my already tired mind, I suddenly got scared. I turned on all the lights inside the car and continued driving home a little faster. I felt like if I looked in the rearview mirror, I would see Debora sitting there.

Once Debbie's body had been found and her ex-lover arrested, the police report was almost immediately available for the media. I got a copy and read it over and over, trying to understand all the tragic details of the case.

Knowing that Jason Griffith had kept her dead body in his garage for a night before he'd decided to hide it elsewhere, I went to the house to get footage of the place where it all began, and where for Debbie, it had all ended. At the time Griffith killed Debbie, there could have been a family next door having dinner, a child doing his or her homework, or a mother putting her baby to sleep. It was a chilling sensation to know what an awful thing had transpired inside those walls. What was it for Jason Griffith? Rage? Revenge? What?

From television shows like *Ghost Whisperer* and *Medium*, to countless films like *The Sixth Sense* and *The Others*, there are a plethora of stories about spirits of the dead who have not "crossed over" for one reason or another.

The Flores-Narvaezes are a Christian family who hadn't given the idea of communication with the dead much consideration, but after Debbie's demise, her mother, Elsie Narvaez, began finding feathers around the home, which she attributed to coming from Debbie, since there are no birds or feather pillows at the house, and the windows were always closed. And feathers, Elsie said, and Celeste had also heard, were a sign from angels. Celeste also found signs. She often saw blue butterflies and ladybugs at times when she was thinking about Debbie. She felt Debbie's presence.

On her Facebook wall, Celeste Flores-Narvaez wrote the following, on May 24, 2011:

"I am stunned, shocked and curious. I was in my room

when I heard a noise in the living room. I went to check it out and found all my sister's pictures and mementoes knocked down on the floor. There was no one but me in the house, and no way for them to have come down on their own. Could it be her, letting me know she's here? I'm deep in thought about it."

According to experts in the paranormal, this sort of activity is supposedly caused by a trapped and tormented spirit, such as that of murder victims, perhaps seeking justice for their lives being taken suddenly.

The day after her public Facebook post, Celeste wrote in a private correspondence, "I think everyone has a sixth sense, some more than others. I sense stuff all the time. And as far as things moving around, this was not the first time. I have the mantel of the chimney filled with her pictures and things. Her couch sits in front of it facing her things. It is her area. Sometimes my dog barks at her things in her area. And sometimes the baby babbles straight at the couch as if there were someone there, as if he's looking at someone sitting on the couch and talking to them. Well, there was always something moving or falling. But this was the first time when all of it fell together at the same time. But I don't feel scared, not at all. I just pray that it's her."

And Celeste was not the only one to receive a "message."

Dancer Tessa Ortiz, who works with magician Rene

Delgadillo as his dancer-assistant, had been Debbie's roommate before Sonya Sonnenberg. "While I was living with her she was going through problems with her restraining order with Jamile," Tessa recalled.

"I was very shocked after her death, but in a way kind of not, because I had a bad feeling that something was going to happen, that something wasn't right." About a month before Debbie's death and disappearance, Tessa said, she'd had a dream, "a very frightening dream. It was very scary." Tessa dreamed that Debbie's dead body was hidden underneath her bed. "In my dream I was terrified. I kept thinking to myself, 'the police are going to think I did it.' After I had that dream, I found out what happened to her, and [that] Blu was telling people at his work [that] the police were going to think he did it. When I woke up the next day I called [Debbie] immediately to make sure she was all right. I didn't tell her [why]. I didn't want to scare her. It was a month before it happened. Now I feel kind of guilty that I didn't tell her about it; maybe she would have taken more precautions."

Not long after her Facebook entry, Celeste sought the advice of renowned psychic Gale St. John, whom Larry King once introduced on his program as "the only psychic who has ever prevented a murder." Gale had once warned the police that a dead girl, whose father had contacted the psychic previously, was telling her to look for her roommate, who was also in peril. The police did so, albeit reluctantly. It turned out the roommate was in danger of being killed by the same person who had murdered the first girl.

Gale St. John, for her part, had often participated in the Internet radio show *Missing in America*, hosted by Marta Sosa out of Minneapolis, Minnesota. The show attempts to find solutions to crimes, through victims' families, investigators, and friends, by putting their cases out there, on the air. Gale is the show's "go-to psychic" on their programs about missing persons. When contacted about appearing on that program so she might speak with Gale St. John, Celeste eagerly agreed.

The show aired live on August 2, 2011. Once everyone was in place, Marta Sosa, the host, asked Celeste about growing up with her little sister, Debora, to start things off on a happy note and ease into the topic. Celeste talked cheerfully about how she and Debbie had played together as children, with games and with their stuffed animals. "We were always loved and cared for. We weren't rich, but we had a lot of fun."

Then the older sister talked about how Debbie had loved to dance and perform as a child, about her success as a cheerleader, and about her desire for attention. "She always spoke her mind. She always stood her ground. And she wanted the world to know who she was."

Celeste and Marta also spoke about the day Debbie

disappeared, right before she was slated to become a lead dancer in the Las Vegas Luxor show, *FANTASY.*

Marta Sosa then asked Celeste what she knew about Debbie's ex-boyfriend, Jason "Blu" Griffith. As she had said before, and others had corroborated, the dancer had been rather secretive about the whole affair. "What she did was tell everybody a little bit of everything so nobody had the whole story," Celeste said.

Psychic Gale St. John had remained silent until this point, but then she said she had to jump in and voice what she was receiving, nonstop. "I really feel, and I have to say this, that your sister knew very well this person was going to be the end of her, but she couldn't stop her emotions. That driving desire, that feeling of 'gotta have it,' it's like a drug addiction. She knew what was going to come of it. She had visions of what would happen, she had dreams, she had impressions, but she put them off, because of her driving desire to have a relationship with this person. It isn't necessarily she thought she could change him as much as she tried to accept him and live with the way he was. He wasn't loyal to her."

Celeste agreed: "No, he wasn't."

The psychic elaborated, as she saw more images. "I see pearls; I see pink pearls."

Celeste was astounded. "Oh my God, she loved pearls. She was always wearing them!"

Gale St. John continued, "I don't know what this means, but she really liked pink. She liked purple, too, but the lavender purple, not the gaudy purple."

The sister was pleasantly surprised. "Yes, she loved pink and lavender! And I never liked them and I wear them now. All of a sudden I surround myself in purple and pink, and I never liked them before. Is there anything she wanted me to know in particular?" she asked Gale St. John.

The psychic wasn't ready to move on to that question yet. She was still working to prove to Celeste that she was really communicating with Debbie. "This is going to sound strange, but a lot of people love roses. She hates them; she likes daisies."

Celeste came alive again: "Yes! She hated roses! She loved daisies!"

"And pearls, she is wearing pearls. She wants you to know that. Pink pearls!"

"Oh my God!" the sister exclaimed again. "Yes, she loved her pearls and she was never without them, her pink pearls!"

"These are things that are important to know, so you see she's really here. The most important things are the things she impresses with you every day, the love and the comfort." Gale St. John then returned to speaking about Debbie's doomed relationship. "She had a good friend that he slept with, and that really hurt. They partied and

DANCING ON HER GRAVE

drank together. She was changing herself and losing a part of herself in the process. The final straw was the cheating with the friend. That was a huge argument. He did drugs, and the other girl did drugs. I don't feel that your sister liked drugs."

Celeste interjected softly, "No, she did not."

And Gale proceeded. "That was a huge letdown for her, and he said a lot of unforgiving things. Your sister was not prone to violence, but he pushed her to the limit and she slapped him. From there it spiraled downward."

After a few beats, Celeste said: "This confirms a lot of what I know, and surmised." And then she asked the most difficult question of all. "Did she go peacefully?"

Gale St. John did not hesitate in her response: "I would say there were moments of suffering. She knew it was over. When the friend was there he was holding her against the wall. I'm not seeing a whole picture but at the last moment she knew. He wasn't letting her have any air." On this the psychic was right on point. Jason Griffith had placed a plastic bag over Debbie's head, and she complained she couldn't breathe. Gale St. John did not know this.

"She did suffer until the moment when she passed out. But she knew. When the friend left, it crossed her mind to leave, but it was too late. Her last thoughts were she should have left."

Marta Sosa then asked Gale St. John if she thought

Debbie Flores-Narvaez's murder had been planned. Some people, like Debbie's high school friend, Tennille Ball, had theorized that Griffith had planned on killing Debbie all along, because he did not want her to testify in court against him for the incident in which he had assaulted her in October 2010.

The psychic now hesitated: "How do I put this? He had feelings of wanting to hurt her severely, and had thought about it. There was a certain amount of pleasure he got from it. Some people are actually remorseful. With him there was no remorse."

The radio show host then turned the talk to Jason "Blu" Griffith's upcoming trial for murder, thinking that perhaps Celeste might be able to draw some strength from this, for the difficult time to come. "The trial," Marta Sosa said. "It's not going to be an easy thing for Celeste."

Now Gale St. John was emphatic, because apparently she was getting urgent messages from Debbie to relate. "Yes, but what she's saying is, it's not important what happens in the way of looking at her life; she's a little angry right now. She's angry right now, and she is saying, 'Everyone thinks I'm dead!' Her attitude is kind of 'Damn-it, don't let that destroy what I am!' Take an item of hers with you, something pink or purple, and think of her today."

Celeste was crying again. "I talk to her every day like she's here."

"That's what she wants. She doesn't want you to think about what happened. It's important to you, it's important to the court, but she's very headstrong."

The sister—who would be at the trial every day—then asked, "Is there anything she wants me to say on her behalf?"

"It's very strange for me to say this, but she takes responsibility for her own actions that led to this. That is not to say that what happened is okay. She's very much that way, in saying I cannot give someone else one hundred percent blame. And I appreciate the fact she is like that. The most important thing she says is, don't hold the grief and the anger because it will turn your life around. Turn it into a positive and not a negative. And she keeps saying, 'OWN IT.'"

Celeste said, knowingly, and one could almost see her nodding, sadly, "I have heard her say those words before."

"That means the grief and the anger, own it. That's how she describes the word. That way that person doesn't win. Are you the one that paints? Who paints?"

Celeste said, "I do."

"She'll come through you. Some artwork is coming from you, because she is going to inspire you with beautiful things. And with work that will draw money and will help fund projects."

Celeste said: "Yes, I have been doing that, donating all the monies to Shade Tree, a center for domestic violence. And I also want her to know her friend Luke who is a lawyer is setting up a scholarship for arts and dance and music in her name."

Gale said, "Well, you and her friends are beginning to own it."

At this point, the topic of the Facebook entries Celeste had written that alluded to poltergeist activity in her home were introduced.

Celeste said that when she'd brought Debbie's things to her home in Atlanta, she'd decided to put a lot of her pictures on the mantel, safely beyond the reach of her dog and her kids. "And on this particular night my kids weren't home and my dog was in the room with me," she recalled. "On this particular night, I heard something. And when I went out there to that area, all her pictures were knocked down. There wasn't an earthquake, and they're not hanging on the wall; there is no way they could fall over. But they were all on the floor."

Gale St. John did not pause this time. "It's her. It's very much your sister, letting you know she's there. And that she's upset and angry still. She is voicing her opinion, as she did so well." And there was a slight moment of laughter from Celeste in recognition of the willful young woman with a mind of her own.

Then Marta Sosa, the show's host, asked psychic Gale St. John again if Debbie had a message for her sister.

"There are so many things that are unknown or unspoken, but don't fear anything," Gale St. John reassured Celeste. "Just understand where it came from. There is a book, maybe a diary."

Celeste said Debbie kept several quote books, and wrote in them. "She also wrote on her computer a lot."

"If you are ever able to read this, read between the lines," the psychic advised. "Read between the lines because I feel she writes about her own death."

Celeste then spoke about another unusual occurrence, which was the lights flickering all over her house. She wanted to know if it was her sister doing that.

Now Gale St. John was emphatic. "Yes! When those lights flicker, give it to her! She has a sense of pride about it! She's worked very hard to do that! Give it to her!"

There was more laughter, then Celeste said, softly, "I will make sure that I do."

NINE

◇◇◇

The Wait

Facebook, for all of its trappings and extraneous nonsense, also seemed a good outlet for Celeste to share her thoughts not only with friends, but with all who knew Debbie. Mostly, though, she seemed to use it as a public outcry, out of impotence and sadness. For instance, on October 4, 2011, Celeste wrote the following Facebook entry:

"I think of her every day. I can't seem to get it out of my mind, what could I have done different to save her? And now as the end of the year grows near and I will have to go back to Vegas to face the worthless shit that took her from us I wonder, what will I do? Will I contain myself? Mentally I'm preparing myself from the start, but how will I really feel when I face him and have the chance to speak my mind in her and my family's behalf?"

In fact, it was altogether possible that the trial verdict, not to mention any potential sentence that Jason Griffith might receive for the murder of her sister, might not be as harsh as she wished. He had not even gone to trial yet by that time. Griffith might be convicted, yes, but most likely of manslaughter, not murder.

The Clark County District Attorney's office already stated that the case did not meet the requirements for a capital punishment case, which required three factors: whether the conviction would stand up under appeal; whether there were aggravating factors; and whether a jury would impose capital punishment. It had to be a case of premeditated murder in order to be considered a capital case.

The sister already knew this, but she wasn't happy about it.

"Yes, I was reading up on the manslaughter sentence in Nevada and it's from four to ten years," she said. "I can promise you that if he gets a sentence of that sort at the end by the judge, I'm going to go absolutely ballistic and out of my mind in that courtroom. The thought of it as I was reading was too much for me to bear. No amount of counseling can hold back my reaction to that sentence. It upsets me thinking about it."

Even knowing that having too strong a reaction inside the courtroom could result in her removal from the court again wasn't enough to deter Celeste. "Contempt in the courtroom would be the least of my worries if that happens," she replied irately. "I'd have to be committed to a mental hospital because I would seriously lose it!" The first time Jason appeared in court, Celeste lost it, and started screaming at him in tears. A security guard had to escort her out of the room.

Once she'd calmed down, Celeste told me over the phone, "I think it's crazy, because he attempted to choke her, the roommate pulled him off, the roommate left, and he continued to choke her. He had time to think."

But what kinds of mitigating factors might be brought up by Jason Griffith's lawyers at trial? Public information officer Jacinto Rivera told us that Jason Griffith was under suicide watch at the jail, even though he was segregated from the general population for his own safety.

Griffith had a history of threatening self-harm. In fact, on November 2, 2010, just over a month before Debbie's murder, a friend of his had contacted the Las Vegas police, saying that he "was concerned for Griffith's welfare because he had received a text message from Griffith that caused [the friend] to believe Griffith was suicidal." According to the report, Patrol Officers were dispatched and responded to Griffith's residence. Griffith was transported to Mountain View Hospital.

Even more surprising was the discovery that Jason Griffith was still married, though his wife had left him years ago. She did not want to disclose her identity, but did, however, offer some background information regarding his violent tendencies both to himself and to others.

Griffith's wife stated that in October 2003, he'd punched her in the face and knocked her out. He'd busted her lip, pinned her down, and said, "If you leave me, I'm going to cut my face." That was before they were married.

She added that he would threaten suicide as a way to try to control her, and that was her breaking point. She had decided to leave once earlier, but then found out she was pregnant and thought she wanted the baby to have a father.

The two married in November 2006 and moved to Nevada in 2007. The woman said Griffith also barricaded himself in the bathroom once, threatening to kill himself. Police officers had had to remove him from the premises.

And then there were the incidents of domestic violence with Debora Flores-Narvaez—three of them—in which he was sometimes the suspect and sometimes the victim. There was no question that the two of them had had a violent relationship. "Records show three previous reports taken under LVMPD," a police report states. "Griffith

The Flores-Narvaez family was not wealthy, but sisters Celeste and Debbie never wanted for anything growing up.

Celeste Flores-Narvaez

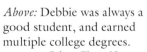

Above: Debbie was always a good student, and earned multiple college degrees.
Celeste Flores-Narvaez

Left: Celeste, Debbie's older sister, never wavered in her own relentless investigation into Debbie's death.
Celeste Flores-Narvaez

Debbie was a devoted aunt to her two nephews, Celeste's sons. The last call she made to her sister was to find out what to get her older nephew for Christmas.

Celeste Flores-Narvaez

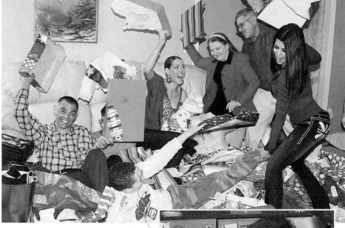

Above: The Flores-Narvaez family during happier times.

Celeste Flores-Narvaez

Right: Debbie and Sonya, her roommate in Las Vegas, where Debbie moved to pursue her dancing career.

Sonya Sonnenberg

Left and below: Debbie often worked with a friend, magician Rene Delgadillo, whose act combined magic and salsa dancing.

Shane O'Neal

Debbie was looking forward to her first solo in the *FANTASY* extravaganza on the Las Vegas Strip.

Carolina Sarassa

MISSING

Debbie Flores Narvaez
www.bringdebbiehome.com

DESCRIPTION

Hispanic
Brown Hair
Brown Eyes
Age: 31
Height: 5'5"
Weight: 125lbs
Missing From: Las Vegas, NV
Last known sighting was on Dec. 12 around 7 p.m., when she left her Vegas home to visit an ex-boyfriend driving her maroon, four-door 1997 Chevrolet Prism.

Anyone with information of her whereabouts is encouraged to contact
Metro's Missing Person Unit at 707-828-2907
or Crime Stoppers at 702-385-5555

Help Us Bring Her Home

Celeste created this missing person's flyer for her sister.

Celeste Flores-Narvaez

Mug shot taken of Debbie during one of her reports of domestic violence.

Howard County Police Station, Maryland

Mug shot of Jason Omar Griffith, Debbie's ex-boyfriend.
Las Vegas Metropolitan Police Department

Griffith awaited his trial at the Clark County jail.
Las Vegas Metropolitan Police Department

Jacinto Rivera, the public information officer for the Las Vegas Metropolitan Police Department.
Carolina Sarassa

Domestic violence activist Rebeca Ferreira.
Stephanie Gonzalez

Experienced prosecutor Marc DiGiacomo had surprises up his sleeve during the trial.

Marc DiGiacomo

Prosecutor Michelle Fleck gave the final summation after the trial.

Michelle Fleck

Defense attorney Abel Yáñez stated that he would file an appeal on behalf of his client.

Abel Yáñez

Celeste took her sister back to their native Puerto Rico to be buried. *Celeste Flores-Narvaez*

Celeste vows to visit Debbie's gravesite often to "make sure she is happy." *Celeste Flores-Narvaez*

was listed as a victim in one, with Flores-Narvaez listed as the suspect. Griffith was listed as the suspect of domestic violence once, and was arrested for battery, domestic violence and coercion once. In both events Flores-Narvaez was listed as the victim."

But if Jason Griffith had such disregard for his own life, would it seem surprising, in hindsight, that he would have so callously obliterated his ex-girlfriend, Debora Flores-Narvaez?

A "dance with death" was Jane Velez-Mitchell's comment about the case during an episode of the *Dr. Phil* show that aired on August 15, 2012, titled: "Murder of a Las Vegas Showgirl."

Four women appeared on this particular program: Jason Griffith's mother and sister, Charlene Davis and Samantha Griffith; and Debbie's mother and sister, Elsie Narvaez and Celeste Flores-Narvaez.

Jane Velez-Mitchell announced at the opening: "This is one of the most gruesome cover-ups I've ever seen."

During the show's opener, one could hear Charlene allege that Debbie was the aggressor. "If my son did kill her, it had to be self-defense," she said.

"It's a story that played out like a Hollywood movie," said Dr. Phil in his ingratiating, soft Southern drawl. "A beautiful Las Vegas showgirl, a cryptic message, and suddenly the stunning dancer goes missing from what was to be the biggest performance of her life. And then the worst possible outcome and a gruesome, gruesome discovery."

Charlene Davis spoke about a black-and-white video her son had recorded that showed Debbie Flores-Narvaez threatening him. Both Charlene and her daughter, Samantha Griffith, alleged that Jason Griffith had never been violent toward a female, nor toward anyone for that matter, in any situation.

But Dr. Phil's production team had found Jason Griffith's ex-wife, as she now refers to herself even though they were separated, and she told a very different story. She did not want her identity revealed but had told Dr. Phil's production team that Griffith had punched her in the face, which the host mentioned during the broadcast.

Dr. Phil asked the mother and sister, "Did Jason kill her?"

Neither denied it, but they both said it was because he felt his life was threatened.

Celeste then went on to describe the gruesome details of her sister's slaying and dismemberment, including how Jason Griffith's roommate, Louis Colombo, had already had to stop Griffith from choking Debbie once, earlier that night, then had to leave the apartment—and returned to find that Griffith had killed her. She described how the two men had first attempted to conceal her sister's body

DANCING ON HER GRAVE

in a large tub of concrete, but when that one proved too unwieldy and started to leak, Griffith had decided to cut Debbie's body in half and place it in two separate tubs instead, which the two roommates then hid in the home of people they knew to be out of the country. "I was so disgusted. I literally wanted to break down that door and just set ablaze the house," Celeste said on air.

On the videotape, Debbie finally tells Jason that if he chooses to engage in battle with her, that legally he will lose.

Debbie was obviously drawing from her degree in law.

At this point, Samantha Griffith mentioned that Debbie had restraining orders.

Dr. Phil again pointed to the differences in weight between aggressor and victim, and to the time it takes to strangle someone, to which Jane Velez-Mitchell replied, "I think you're right on the money, Dr. Phil. Do you know how long it takes to choke somebody to death? It doesn't happen instantly. You've got to do this for at least a minute. So when you say self-defense, there were many moments during that minute of choking her that he could've backed off and said, 'you know, I'm going to stop now.' He didn't. I think this is a very angry guy. He had a lot of rage at her. So I will say that."

Jason Griffith's mother didn't dispute that about her son. In fact, she said her son had sought help for his issues with anger and depression on numerous occasions but had been turned away.

Dr. Phil said, "Are you saying the system failed him?"

Charlene Davis voiced the answer that made the most sense of all: "The system failed both of them."

But that wasn't enough of an answer for Celeste. As she said to Charlene: "Even if your son asked for help, he had no right to kill her."

Dr. Phil turned to Jane Velez-Mitchell and asked her, "Jane, have you heard anything here today that changes your point of view or perspective or how you'll report on this story?"

She replied, "Well, if he was so afraid of her, why did he let her in that night? And she must've had a foreshadowing of this, because she sent that text to her mom saying if anything happened to me, please look to him. So these were two highly volatile people who were in a very self-destructive dance with death."

The year 2012 was a good one for me professionally. As a news reporter, I knew that if I wanted to continue growing in my career, I needed to relocate.

It had already happened before when I moved from Florida to Texas and then Nevada. My next move had to be Los Angeles, California.

For the Spanish TV market, Los Angeles is numero uno. I was very happy anchoring the late news in Vegas, but when the opportunity came along to be part of a new national network in California, I had to jump at it.

During this time, Debora's murder trial was still being postponed. The family, Diana, and I were impatiently waiting for it.

Every time Jason Griffith had a calendar call known as a "status hearing" about the trial, our hopes were to have a final date. It ended up happening two years after I moved to Los Angeles.

Fortunately for us, our local affiliate station covered the trial, and I kept in touch with my reporter colleagues, who were always so open to sharing the inside information with us. The day the trial started, I received a lot of phone calls from people aware of my continuing interest in the case.

By 2013, we were still waiting for a trial, but the news of Debbie's death had faded away. Nobody was covering the case anymore. Sadly, it had become another murder statistic in Sin City. The news reporters didn't even cover every time Jason had a calendar call for his trial. After all, it was only more of the "same old same old." Even the postponements were old news; the *Las Vegas World News* ran the headline: "Court records now indicate that the trial has been postponed. It is the SIXTH postponement."

On six instances, a trial date had been set for Jason "Blu" Griffith, charged with murder in the death of his former girlfriend, Debora Flores-Narvaez.

There were many factors that contributed to the multiple postponements. Mind you, it caused a lot of distress for the family, having to hear the word "postponed" over and over again. To the justice system, it was merely a case number; to the Flores-Narvaez family, it was their daughter, their sister, their dear Debbie.

The first delay came because the case had been assigned to district judge Donald Mosley, who retired in early 2012. The case was reassigned to district judge Kathleen Delaney.

Various other delays were due to problems obtaining documents. A lot of the documents the public defenders presented as evidence during the trial came from Maryland, where Debbie lived prior to her move to Las Vegas. The defense attorney later said that what made it more difficult to get them was the power of a subpoena, which only works within the state. The defense wanted to have with them the previous restraining orders some of her ex-boyfriends had imposed on Debora, including a 2005 police report from one of Debbie's ex-boyfriends, who was actually a police officer himself in Maryland. The delay in obtaining the documents caused the trial to be postponed more than once.

The trial also had to be delayed once because the medical expert with whom the defense attorneys were working became very ill, so they had to file a motion to find a new expert.

It was all very frustrating, especially for Celeste, a single mother who flew to Las Vegas multiple times only to find out her sister's murder trial was being postponed over and over again.

The prosecution and the defense were always polite over the phone, but the answer always came to, "We can only discuss the case after it's over." Of course they couldn't discuss it without divulging anything about their plans of action. More than two years had passed, and it wasn't over. Those of us in the media continued to wait for the story; Celeste waited to get justice for her sister.

After putting a lot of thought into it, I decided to write a letter to Jason Griffith. Yes, to Debbie's murderer. It was an attempt to get into his head, so to speak, even though I didn't think he would tell us the absolute truth.

All I knew was that his girlfriend, Agnes Roux, the woman he'd claimed was the true love of his life, wasn't visiting him in jail. I knew that he was in solitary confinement, isolated, because the jail officers were worried he might do something to harm himself.

So on April 23, 2013, I sent this letter to Jason, hoping to get a reply.

Hi Jason,

How are you? I am writing this letter because I want to get to know the real Jason, the dancer, the star, not the person who is on trial. I know you studied dance at Juilliard and I want to know about your passion for the dance, and your craft and love of music.

I am not sure if you remember me. My name is Carolina. We spoke over the phone more than a year ago.

The day I'd met Celeste for the first time, she had given me Jason Griffith's phone number. I'd called and spoken to him, but he hadn't wanted to give me an on-camera interview to talk about his ex-girlfriend's disappearance.

I am a journalist, but also a human being. Life has taught me there [are] always two or more sides to a story. There is no such thing as black or white to me.

I am writing a book about the incident. As you might know, it has been very easy to find out more about Debora, her childhood, her life.

I would like to be fair and know more about Jason, the father, the friend. I don't want to know about the case or want you to tell me details about it.

I want to know if they are treating you OK there, if you feel better now that you are not isolated. Are you lonely? How do you pass the time?

I don't want to describe you as someone you are not. I want to be fair to you.

> *I look forward to*
> *hearing back from you!*
> *Carolina*

He never answered, nor acknowledged my letter through his attorneys.

TEN

◇◇◇

The Trial

As she did in many of her posts, Celeste announced the date set for her sister's murder trial on Facebook:

"Finally, finally, finally, it's official. My little sister's Debbie Flores murder trial will start May 5th."

It was 2014, and it had been three and a half years since Debbie's dreams had ended abruptly. It had been over three long years that her ex-boyfriend Jason Griffith had sat in jail, awaiting trial for her murder. I'd kept abreast of any progress in the scheduling of the trial, and Celeste had been despairing now for years, although at times, on Facebook, she tried to joke and reach out to her friends.

It had also been more than three long years for the Flores-Narvaez family to wait for justice to be served. Nothing could bring Debbie back to their next Christmas celebration, but knowing that the man who'd ended her life would pay for what he did could close an important chapter in their lives.

But would he actually pay? Would the verdict turn out the way the bereaved family hoped and expected?

The trial finally began at 1:30 P.M. on May 5, 2014. This was a big case for local news coverage in Las Vegas. It was a dramatic case that had not only moved the community but had also generated high television ratings. Every local station and newspaper had featured stories about Debbie Flores-Narvaez's murder when it had happened. Now that the wheels of justice were finally turning, it was no different. The court was filled with reporters. Meanwhile, Debbie's older sister had become very media savvy. While everyone waited for opening statements to start, Celeste conducted interviews with several local Las Vegas reporters who had not seen her in more than a year. They knew her, though. They knew how relentless she had been in the pursuit of justice of some sort for her little sister.

The trial took place in the Regional Justice Center. It started with a calendar call, a normal procedure in court, and both prosecution and defense stated that they were finally ready to begin.

Clark County District Court judge Kathleen E. Delaney presided. Delaney is in her forties, with dark hair and soft features. According to her biography on the

Department 25, Eighth Judicial District Court, site, she's been a practicing attorney since 1990 and was elected to the district court in 2008. She took the bench in Department 25 on January 5, 2009. Judge Delaney was assigned to hear criminal, civil, and business court matters, and handled all appeals from the state's Foreclosure Mediation Program.

The courtroom where *Nevada vs. Jason Omar Griffith* took place was Judge Delaney's own courtroom. Judges are granted the liberty of decorating their courtrooms after their own fashion, and Delaney had covered all the courtroom walls with photographs of dogs, specifically basset hounds, to call attention to the plight of homeless canines in Las Vegas. (Basset hounds appear to be favorites of Judge Delaney's, since her own judge's site shows a photo of her surrounded by her own pooches of that breed.)

Before trial began, the judge had signed an order granting immunity to Louis Colombo, Jason Griffith's roommate. While Louis could have been considered an accomplice, since he had certainly aided Griffith in the concealment of Debbie's body, the prosecution felt it was worth making a deal. Louis Colombo would be a key witness for them, and his testimony would prove crucial to their case.

The judge interviewed more than eighty prospective jurors, until finally, three days later, the jury pool was finally narrowed down to the twelve men and women who would decide Jason Griffith's fate.

On murder cases, there are usually two attorneys assigned for the prosecution by the District Attorney's Office, and two for the defense.

The lead prosecutor was chief deputy district attorney Marc DiGiacomo. A seasoned attorney with fifteen years' experience as prosecutor, and ten on the Major Violators Unit, DiGiacomo obtained his law degree from the prestigious Jesuit Fordham University of New York. DiGiacomo looks like an academic, with a gray beard and a halo of gray hair, resembling an older, taller, and more massive Richard Dreyfuss.

He would be working alongside prosecutor Michelle Fleck, formerly of Special Victims Unit, who had then taken DiGiacomo's place before moving on to the prosecution division. Fleck is an attractive blond woman with a finishing school look but the firm manner of a police detective. DiGiacomo refers to her as "an excellent litigator." Fleck has a healthy respect for DiGiacomo's skills as well. "Marc is brilliant, he is everything a prosecuting attorney should be," she said about her colleague, and now partner in this important trial.

The defense attorneys were Abel Yáñez and Jeff Banks.

Abel Yáñez is a dashing Argentinian in his early forties, with black hair, green eyes, and a Grecian profile. His parents moved to the United States during the Argentinian dictatorship, a time when many families fled the country. He remembers his parents always talking and complaining about how the government was violating their civil rights, how they were all over "people's business."

Griffith's case had been randomly assigned to Yáñez, and he, as the lead attorney, chose to work with Jeff Banks. They had worked together on criminal cases before, and Yáñez felt Banks would be his perfect partner. He knew that Banks, a compassionate man also in his early forties with children of his own, would work tirelessly for the defense.

Yáñez opened his private practice in 2014, about six months before the trial started. He could have just handed the case to Jeff and a new public defendant, but since he knew so many details, he continued doing it pro bono (at no charge). It was a case he thought he could win, he said, or at least get a reduced sentence.

Yáñez told the jurors they would hear about the "violence, property crimes, stalking, threats, harassment all by Debbie Flores against Mr. Griffith as well as acts of battery and weapons."

On May 8, 2014, Jason Griffith listened intently as the judge issued instructions to the jurors. Griffith, very well dressed in a suit, with a slight beard and looking a couple of pounds lighter than he had in 2011, sat next to his attorneys. Throughout the trial, he seemed to be trying to avoid eye contact, especially with Celeste. His expression, however, was impassive.

Judge Kathleen Delaney told the jury that it was their duty "to apply the rules of law the facts as you find them from the evidence," and said, "Regardless of any opinion you may have as to what the law ought to be, it would be a violation of your oath to base a verdict upon any other view of the law than that given in the instructions of the Court."

She explained what the charges were against Jason Griffith, pointing out that the fact he'd been indicted for the crime was only "a formal method of accusing a person of a crime and is not of itself any evidence of his guilt." She went on to say that his indictment charged him as follows: "on or about the 12th day of December, 2010 at and within the County of Clark, State of Nevada, the Defendant committed the offense of MURDER, to wit: did then and there feloniously, without authority of law, and with malice aforethought, kill Debora Flores-Narvaez, a human being, by strangulation and/or compression and/or means unknown."

Judge Delaney defined the crime of murder as "the unlawful killing of a human being, with the malice aforethought, whether express or implied" and gave the jurors the legal definition of "malice aforethought" (aka premeditation): "Malice aforethought means the intentional doing of a wrongful act without legal cause or excuse or what the law considers adequate provocation. The condition of mind described as malice aforethought may arise, not alone from anger, hatred, revenge, or from particular ill will, spite or grudge toward the person killed, but may result from any unjustifiable or unlawful motive or purpose to injure another, which proceeds from a heart fatally bent on mischief or with reckless disregard or consequences and social duty. Malice aforethought does not imply deliberation or the lapse of any considerable time between the malicious intention to injure another and the actual execution of the intent but denotes rather an unlawful purpose and design in contradistinction to accident and mischance."

Judge Kathleen Delaney further explained what is meant by premeditation, or "malice murder": "Express malice is that deliberate intention unlawfully to take away the life of a fellow creature. [. . .] Malice may be implied when no considerable provocation appears." Perhaps most importantly, the judge also explained exactly how a crime qualified as first degree: "Murder of the first degree is murder which is perpetrated by means of any kind of willful, deliberate, and premeditated killing. All three (3) elements—willfulness, deliberation, and premeditation—must be proven beyond a reasonable doubt before an accused can be convicted of first-degree murder. [. . .] Murder of the Second Degree is murder with malice aforethought, but without the admixture of premeditation and deliberation. All murder which is not murder of the first degree is murder of the second degree."

Then, district attorney Marc DiGiacomo gave his opening statement.

"This is one of the most intense searches in modern Las Vegas history," DiGiacomo said.

Jurors heard from various witnesses who testified about the days following Debora Flores-Narvaez's disappearance and the search effort by Las Vegas police and her family; they heard from her roommate, Sonya, and from her sister, Celeste, who flew to Las Vegas from Atlanta and testified about what occurred when she contacted Griffith regarding her sister's whereabouts: "He showed little concern. I felt like he was lying about not knowing where she was."

Defense attorney Jeff Banks anticipated that the prosecution would present police photographs to the jurors as evidence during the trial, by saying, "They will show you pictures, and they will be gruesome and they will be shocking. But that does not change the fact that he was scared and he was afraid that she was violent, and Jason Griffith was defending himself on December 12, 2010." Jason Griffith's lawyers asked that the jury consider the man's state of mind, suggesting that he had been acting in self-defense.

"She was a violent stalker who had repeatedly harassed him," Banks told the jury.

The prosecution disagreed, saying there was no evidence to support a self-defense claim. The prosecution spent more than an hour talking about Jason's affairs with different women. "Griffith tried to hide his crime and maintain his life as a Cirque du Soleil performer along with his relationship with another woman," DiGiacomo refuted, referring obliquely to Agnes Roux, one of the other women in Jason Griffith's life during his time with Debbie. (Agnes was Debbie's main competition with Griffith, since Debora knew he had deep feelings for the redheaded dancer. Even before her murder, the couple had many arguments because of the relationship Griffith had with the *Zumanity* dancer.)

Then came a most difficult task for the jury. As the defense had expected, the prosecution did show the jury graphic autopsy photographs of Debbie. It was incredibly jarring to see the young woman who had once been a model and dancer as a dismembered corpse on a video screen. Pictures of her torso and severed legs were part of the gruesome evidence the prosecuting attorneys showed the jury. The autopsy pictures were shown early on during the opening statements, so the jurors had a clear understanding of the magnitude of the dismemberment of Debbie's body.

Prosecutor Marc DiGiacomo told the jury that evidence over the next several days would prove that Griffith was not only guilty but had intentionally killed his ex-lover by asphyxiating her with a plastic bag over her head—and had twice tried to dispose of her body in six hundred pounds of cement.

"The problem for Mr. Griffith is, it's painfully apparent that he never does anything alone," DiGiacomo told the jury, referring to Griffith having enlisted the help of his friend and roommate, Louis Colombo, which would prove to be his downfall. DiGiacomo explained how Louis had witnessed Griffith as he "sawed the legs off [Flores-Narvaez's] corpse to fit her remains in two smaller concrete-filled tubs that weighed less." Her legs! Although Jason Griffith chopped up his ex-lover's legs out of expediency and in order to fit her in the tub filled with concrete where he intended to conceal her body, perhaps it was a subconscious act of the worst kind. There was something especially disturbing about this image, Griffith's horrific treatment of the dancer's main artistic instrument.

The next day, on Friday, May 9, 2014, Kalae Casorso, one of Jason Griffith's (many) former girlfriends, took the stand. During her testimony, she told the jury how she had demanded to know what was in the heavy big blue plastic tub of gray rocky material that Griffith and his roommate, Louis Colombo, wanted to store at her home. This is when she learned the truth.

"I asked what the heck it was. He asked if I really wanted to know, and I said yes. He kind of looked at me and said it was Debbie," testified Kalae.

She said she felt "confused and stunned" at this revelation. The prosecution asked her twice why she didn't call police.

"But you don't call the police at all?" asked DiGiacomo, perhaps anticipating how the defense might drill Casorso.

"Not at that time, no," answered Kalae.

"And you knew you could get into trouble, right?"

If she had knowingly helped to hide Debora's remains, Kalae could have been charged with "accessory after the fact," which is often not considered an accomplice but is treated as a separate offender. Punishment for an accessory after the fact—basically anyone who intentionally helps an offender evade apprehension or prosecution—is always less than for the principal offender.

Kalae said, "I feared what happened to the woman I knew as Debbie Flores could happen to me."

She told jurors that she'd broken off her relationship with Griffith after spotting him with Debbie Flores-Narvaez on Valentine's Day, 2010. That seemed to be a pattern with Jason Griffith: a current girlfriend would either see him with another woman, or find out about another woman, and the relationship was over.

Despite their breakup, however, Kalae went on to say that she still heard frequently from Griffith, and that he would often complain to her about Debbie.

Las Vegas Metropolitan Police Department detective Dan Long testified in court later that same day. He spoke about the moment he realized Jason Griffith and Louis Colombo had done something horrible to Debbie Flores-Narvaez, recalling his conversation with Louis about becoming a witness for the prosecution if he wanted to save himself.

"I made a comment during the interview and said, as long as there wasn't anything weird with the body. And alarms went off, visual alarms went off, and my partner and I knew at that time, 'okay, they did something to this body,'" said the detective.

Jason Griffith showed little reaction to the testimony. He simply continued to scratch the left side of his head as he listened and patiently sat next to his attorneys in the courtroom during Detective Long's testimony.

Later that night, after court had adjourned, Celeste posted on Facebook about her rage at Griffith's calm courtroom demeanor:

"Shaking from head to toe uncontrollably with so much rage, hate and anger. Tears rolling down my face with the horror that I just saw. The torture she faced, the way she was rid and disposed of and planned to be forgotten for no one to ever see or find. I can only look and stare at evil's face. . . . Evil itself shows No reaction, no remorse, no emotion. No sorrow. Nothing! Just a tall, proud stance. He feels my livid and furious stare and then he attempts to return the favor back only to lose, look down, shake his head in disbelief of the nerve I have for him! Amazing to me, completely shocked at his response to me and the confidence evil has with no regrets. My head is spinning, knots in my stomach and feeling weak. Stress, anger and pain have consumed me entirely. Worst thing in life is feeling helpless. That I cannot do anything at all. To sit. Sit and wait. . . . Wait for justice to be served. Not by your own hand but by someone else's and not know the sentencing yet. I keep asking myself, how? How the hell am I still doing this? How is it I'm still moving forward? How? Begging and praying for strength. God I'm reaching for you."

On Monday, May 12, 2014, after a weekend's rest, the jury was again called to appear for the second week of opening arguments at 10:30 A.M.

Everyone had expected Jason Griffith to take the stand, but instead, the jurors listened to the testimony from crime scene technicians and forensic investigators.

The jury was exposed again to the images of Debbie's severed legs and torso after crime scene investigators had removed them from the tub of cement in preparation for the autopsy, which was performed the day after her remains were found.

Dr. Larry Simmons, a forensic pathologist with the Clark County Coroner's Office who had performed more than eight thousand autopsies during his career, was one of the individuals to take the stand. "She had both her legs amputated away from the rest of her body," he told the court.

"So they were severed. They were amputated at the hip and then there was an attempted amputation at the left arm through the shoulder area."

During this forensic testimony, as he had the previous week, Griffith looked straight ahead, impassive and emotionless, even as the prosecutors showed the gruesome pictures of Debbie's dismembered body. The photos did not appear to sit well with the members or the jury; a couple almost jumped out of their seats, and some covered their mouths with their hands. Some of the women just looked away. Some of the jurors gasped, and others were visibly shaken. Tears rolled down Celeste's and her mother's faces as other crime scene analysts also described in detail the condition in which they had found Debora's body. As a news reporter, one would assume I am used to seeing and hearing about horrific cases, but it is very difficult to even write about this; I cannot imagine what her family felt as they saw those pictures.

"Once the first container was open, we found a head, and a torso, and arms," said Dan Holstein, Metro crime scene analyst, adding that he found a pair of legs in the second container. The CSI analyst was referring to the bags inside the storage tubs where Griffith and Colombo had placed the body parts.

It was a long day at the courthouse. The jury also heard from the employees at Walmart where Jason Griffith had been captured on surveillance video purchasing items like duct tape and cement, as well as from employees at the locations where he'd rented the U-Haul truck.

The following day, May 13, 2014, was even more significant. The prosecution concluded its arguments with the key witness, the man who saw it all: Jason Griffith's best friend and roommate, Louis Colombo.

Louis Colombo, a tall, heavyset man of thirty-five who wore his long hair combed back in a ponytail, took the stand with a palpable sense of guilt. Throughout his more than two and half hours of testimony, his eyes filled up with genuine tears as he gave details of Debbie Flores-Narvaez's tragic ending. In contrast, Jason Griffith did not cry and continued to show no emotion even as his friend described what happened to his ex-lover.

Louis remembered with what seemed to be true remorse the moment he left the apartment knowing Griffith and Debbie had been fighting to the point he witnessed Griffith grab her with both hands on her neck. Prosecutors asked Louis to demonstrate the manner in which he'd witnessed Griffith choking Debbie on the day she died. Louis stood up and showed exactly how Jason Griffith had had his hands wrapped around Debbie's neck before he left their apartment on December 12, 2010. Louis Colombo practically acted out the murder itself, and it was hair-raising.

Confessing that he hadn't wanted to get his good friend in trouble, Louis took everyone in the courtroom step-by-step from the moment he left the apartment until they finally disposed of Debora's body. He claimed to have left the two of them fighting but said that when he returned, he found Debbie dead with a plastic grocery shopping bag over her head.

He said that Griffith told him he'd been afraid Debbie was about to call an ambulance, because she was having trouble breathing, when Griffith approached her from behind and choked her to death.

"I saw Debbie lying on the ground," Louis Colombo said.

"Did she appear alive?" the prosecutor asked.

"No, she appeared dead."

"How could you tell?"

"She wasn't moving," Louis responded.

The prosecutors asked him directly how he and Jason Griffith had gotten rid of her body. The roommates had carried Debbie's body to the bathtub so the dismembering would not leave blood traces.

"Who does the cutting?" DiGiacomo asked.

"Jason," he replied.

"What does he use?" asked the prosecutor again.

"A handsaw," Louis answered.

"Were you able to see what it is that he was cutting?" the prosecutor asked.

"I didn't look. I just held the leg and closed my eyes and turned away," Louis said.

"When it was done, did you see what condition the body was in? What did you see?"

"The limbs were cut off at the hip and there was a deep cut into one of the arms. I think the left arm."

Louis Colombo stated the two had to go buy air fresheners and bleach to cover up the smell. "The smell still haunts me to this day," Louis said.

"Every time I heard a siren I would get anxiety," he said. "I could feel Debbie inside the house. I thought I would see her." He'd known Debbie, after all, and had often seen her at the apartment he'd shared with Jason Griffith.

Debbie's mother and sister sat through the testimony. Debbie's mother used a handkerchief often to wipe her tears as she listened to the terrible details of her daughter's death.

The prosecution rested.

ELEVEN

◇◇◇

The Killer Takes the Stand

On Wednesday, May 14, 2014, Jason Griffith took the stand for the first day of what would turn out to be several days' worth of testimony. The accused killer wore an elegant black suit, as he had every day of the trial, and he looked confident, as if he was about to play his trump card and convince the court that he was actually a victim in this case.

After the strong set of witnesses presented by the prosecution, Griffith had obviously decided to take the stand despite knowing that testifying could open him to potentially damaging cross-examination by prosecutors. It would be his only way of avoiding a Murder One conviction, his only way to explain, as he tried to do with the detectives upon first being arrested, that it had all happened "in the heat of the moment" and was not a pre-meditated act.

When questioned by his defense attorneys over the next few days of testimony, Jason Griffith also appeared very emotional, unlike during his previously stoic appearances in the courtroom. Now he cried, clasped his hands to his face, closed his eyes, and took long pauses as if he was looking for the right words to describe Debbie's final moments.

Despite these actions, however, it was noted that there were no visible tears.

Earlier that Wednesday, before Jason Griffith took the stand, Debbie's ex-boyfriend Jamile McGee also testified for the defense. He told the court that Debbie was a violent person—even though she was the one who had won a $250,000 civil judgment against him in April 2010, claiming that she'd suffered scarring as a result of an assault by Jamile in which he kicked her stomach, dragged her from her car, and held her hostage in his apartment while continuing to beat her.

Once Jason Griffith took the stand—visibly agitated and pausing to compose himself—he told the jury how "clingy" Debbie had been and how he'd felt harassed by her since she was constantly coming to his house and work and wanting to spend time with him.

Griffith told the court how he'd had to call 911 many

times while they were together, as Debbie sometimes refused to leave his home. He said on one occasion, a police officer even laughed at him for complaining about "a hot girl" wanting to be with him, and he said Debora had played to that. "She would ridicule me. She would say, 'You're a man, they're not going to believe you. They are never going to believe that I'm doing anything to you. Why do you keep calling them? They are not going to help you,'" Griffith said.

Griffith was not lying about having called 911 on Debbie. In fact, jurors heard fourteen separate 911 calls Griffith made to Las Vegas and North Las Vegas police asking them for help with his girlfriend. He alleged that when Debbie was mad, she would send him hundreds of text messages and call him many times in a row. "It escalated to thirty text messages a day, forty phone calls a day. It was almost laughable how many phone calls were coming in."

"Any time I pulled back, she'd get really intense," he testified, saying that Debbie handwrote on his car the words: *"I will kill you before I let another bitch have you. I will find you wherever you hide. Love always, your Destiny."*

He said again, "Whenever I try to disengage or pull away or attempt to ignore it, if I don't cater to the phone calls, it gets violent. She starts getting really angry."

Both the defense and the prosecution had been trying

their hardest to gather the best evidence possible for their cases. Both found good pieces of it in Griffith's computer, which was linked to his iPhone, his personal phone.

Defense attorney Abel Yáñez looked at his client's phone record and said he was amazed to confirm how many text messages and phone calls Debora made to Griffith within twenty-four hours.

"When I first saw the record, I thought it was a mistake. I said, how can a human being text so many times in a day?" But then, he said, he realized it was accurate. Debbie really had been bombarding him with attention.

But prosecutor Michelle Fleck painted a very different picture.

"You have to look at the text messages in context so you can see the progression, and Debbie's anger," she said later, after the trial. "It was based upon very specific behavior by him. For instance, he would be in a hotel room with a woman when they were supposed to go out on a date. And there were dozens of women!" said the prosecutor. "There was a girl in makeup, and another girl in wardrobe," Fleck said. During Jason Griffith's testimony, he also admitted that in addition to his relationship with Debbie, he'd been sleeping with two other female colleagues from the show *LOVE* at the time, as well as seeing a fourth woman, the dancer from the Cirque du Soleil show *Zumanity*, Agnes Roux.

Griffith said that Debbie knew about Agnes, and that

they'd considered a three-way relationship, but it had never developed.

"One time, in particular, Debbie couldn't find him, and then she [became] worried, then angry, and then worried again. And it was because they had plans and he was basically torturing her," Fleck said. She even dismissed the 911 calls. "If you go through the times he called 911, he is laughing, he is never scared, he is doing it because he wants attention. After one time he called 911 he text messaged her, 'Makeup sex?' He was using one of the busiest metropolitan dispatches in the country for his personal relationship counseling."

Prosecutor Fleck seemed to have a great deal of respect for the victim. "That girl was true blue when it came to Jason Griffith," she added. "Debbie was too smart for him. She was motivated, strong, passionate, interested in pursuing her own goals and dreams, and helping him with his career. Debbie's problem was [that] she was a truth seeker."

The next day, Thursday, May 15, 2014, Jason Griffith once again took the stand.

"Yeah, hell yeah, hell yeah and I'm scared, scared of this," he said of testifying, not to mention what the outcome of the verdict might be, as well as any possible sentence.

Griffith spent almost five hours that Thursday telling the jury how threatened he'd felt by Debbie and explaining how during the fight that led to her death, she'd told him she was going to kill him and then herself if he continued his relationship with Agnes Roux.

"'You don't give a fuck about me. You don't care about me,'" Griffith said Debbie told him. "'That's why I brought it with me,'" meaning the gun Griffith claimed he thought she'd had. "'I'm gonna kill you and kill myself.'"

He continued, "When she hits me, all these other times she has hit me, I'm in a position where I can get away. I'm in a position where I can just run. There is a hit, I can stand up and move. I'm sitting on the floor, and she's over me, and hits me in the face."

According to Griffith, during their heated argument, Debbie reached for her cream-colored purse, where he believed she had a gun. (She didn't. In fact, there's no evidence to show she ever owned a gun or carried any kind of weapon that day. "She never had a gun," prosecutor Michelle Fleck said later. "Nobody who knew her thought she ever had a gun.")

But Griffith nonetheless said, on the stand: "I want to stop her from getting to the purse," as he alleged that he'd been defending himself against a woman he thought was armed. "I think she's reaching for the gun in her purse, but I have no way to know," Griffith testified. "I was telling her to stop. I pull her back toward me. She says, 'I'm going to fucking kill you. I'm going to fucking kill you,'" Griffith said, describing how Debbie, who was also very agile and athletic, kicked the heels of her high black boots against his bare shins and threw her head back against the bridge of his nose as he held her tightly from behind.

As he held her, he said he pleaded with her to stop, that he didn't want to fight her.

"I thought she was listening to me, because she wasn't moving anymore," he said. "She wasn't scratching me, or gasping for air."

He told the jurors he grabbed her from behind, and held her up in the air as he fell backward. Jason Griffith demonstrated this with all the grace and agility of a dancer. He said Debbie's hair was in his face as he pleaded with her to stop fighting.

"I didn't understand what happened. I thought she was going to get up," he said on the stand. Griffith said he thought Debbie had finally calmed down, but she wasn't saying anything, or moving.

"I sat there for ten minutes waiting for her to get up. I'm praying, 'please God she's going to get up, she's going to be ok, she's going to move, she's going to get up,'" Griffith said.

"Do you stay in the studio? Do you leave? What are you doing?" Abel Yáñez, the defense attorney, asked.

At that point, Griffith said, he left. Leaving Debbie's lifeless body in his apartment, Griffith said that he instead went to see his new girlfriend, Agnes, the woman he called the "love of his life," and acted as "if nothing had happened." He did not tell Agnes what happened to Debora.

"'I'm going to spend the rest of my life in jail because no one's going to believe me,'" he said he thought. He said he didn't call the police because he was frustrated about how they never took him seriously, claiming the officers always made fun of him, telling him a beautiful woman couldn't be dangerous. "It was not my first thought to call these people who never believe. Metro is, shoot first and ask questions later. I'm not calling them with a dead body in my house," he said.

Griffith said it was his roommate, Louis Colombo, who later put the plastic bag over Debbie's face, to determine if she was breathing. But Louis had earlier testified that he'd found Debbie's body with the plastic bag over her head already. Griffith's explanation made no sense. Why on earth would Louis Colombo place a bag over his roommate's ex-lover's head?

Griffith also claimed that it was Louis who'd sawed off Debbie's legs, disputing testimony from his former roommate, who said that Griffith had done the sawing.

The biggest contradiction was Louis's testimony of how Griffith told him he killed Debora. According to Louis, Griffith told him he'd grabbed her by the base of her throat, then approached her from behind and choked her to death.

Jason Griffith disagreed—he said it happened as they were arguing and he tried to calm her down. According to him, Debbie's head had somehow become accidentally wedged in his elbows as they fell backward on the floor of his studio apartment.

Toward the end of his testimony on May 15, Griffith explained how and why they got rid of her body, now in the bathtub.

"Eventually it's going to start to smell, so we talked about covering it, and the idea comes to cover it with concrete. We take the body and start putting it in bags."

Shortly after this, both sides, the prosecutors and the defense, rested for the day. Jason Griffith was expected back in the courtroom at 9:30 A.M. to finish his testimony. The prosecutors had yet to question him.

The past two weeks had been extremely difficult for the family, and even for those of us who unfortunately only got to meet Debbie after her death. I had difficulty sleeping, and fell asleep thinking of Debora's last moments of life.

TWELVE

◇◇◇

Jason Griffith's Trial by Fire

Friday, May 16, 2014, was a difficult day in court for Jason Griffith. He shed no tears, but the prosecution's cross-examination of Griffith's testimony lasted almost all day, exposing to the jury that the killer on trial had not been telling the whole story.

The prosecutor, district attorney Marc DiGiacomo, was unrelenting. He started off by asking, rhetorically: "You have no reason to fabricate to your friends, to your other girls? Statements about Debbie being crazy and not actually being truthful about the fact that you're a coward as it relates to her, that you're a liar as it relates to her, and all of those other things you said to her?" The defense raised an objection and the judge sustained it.

Marc DiGiacomo continued: "Let me rephrase. You are a liar, correct?" asked the prosecutor.

Griffith replied in the affirmative. "Yes, sir," he said.

"And when you want something you are more than willing to lie about it."

"Yes, sir."

"You're more than willing to say 'on my sons,' this is true?" DiGiacomo already knew Griffith had two sons.

"If necessary, yes, I have done that."

"Does this oath mean anything to you, sir?"

Griffith didn't reply, as his attorney objected and the judge sustained it.

Jason Griffith had told the jury about the threatening note he'd found on his car, handwritten by Debbie. This note was a piece of evidence presented by his attorneys to portray him as a victim, not a murderer.

"*I will kill you before I let another bitch have you. I will find you wherever you hide. Love always, your Destiny*," the note read.

Griffith apparently hadn't counted on the prosecutor's rebuttal. DiGiacomo was able to use text messages found synced from the defendant's iPhone to his computer that showed Griffith knew in spring 2010 that the letter had actually been written by his roommate, Louis Colombo, and that it had been meant as a joke.

The text message from Louis said, "Are you still mad

at me? Like I said I didn't mean to make you upset. I thought we'd be able to laugh about it. I didn't think for a second that you'd think it was really her. The letter was so outrageous and in my handwriting. I'm really sorry it caused you grief."

Griffith had replied to Louis with another text: "It wasn't a funny joke at all. She had just said something like that on the phone."

On the stand, Griffith seemed shaken by prosecutor DiGiacomo's discovery, but he composed himself. "I took that note very seriously," he stated on the stand. "I believed that she wrote it. As I said in the text message, she just said something like that on the phone. I had no reason to fabricate that at the time. She had just said something like that on the phone." Griffith then turned to the jury.

"You are a coward, correct?" DiGiacomo said, now getting angry.

Griffith's attorneys objected. "Sustained!" said Judge Delaney.

During an intense day of questioning, the prosecutors got Griffith to admit he'd still contacted Debbie for sex, even during the time she was supposedly harassing him. A portrait was beginning to emerge of Griffith as a sex addict.

"This woman, I've got to imagine, has been torturing

you since February or March 2010, who has finally left you alone for the better part of two weeks. You think it's a good idea to Facebook her?" asked the prosecutor.

"It's her birthday," responded Griffith sheepishly.

DiGiacomo could barely hide a smirk. "Would you agree with me you were having sex with so many women you had to tell a lot of lies to keep it up?"

"No," Griffith replied.

Prosecutors disagreed, producing text message records dating back several years that they said showed Griffith had lied to a lot of women, including a dancer named Agnes.

Griffith said that Agnes was his girlfriend when Debbie died, and that hours after Debbie's death, he'd gone to a hotel to see Agnes.

"Did you tell Agnes [that] Debbie left town and that was why she was no longer in your life?" DiGiacomo asked.

"Never in that much detail," Griffith replied. At this point, Griffith was lying. He had not yet told Agnes Roux that he had murdered Debbie.

Everyone who knew him said that Griffith had seemed okay, even happy in the days and weeks after Debbie's disappearance. Prosecutors questioned him as to why witnesses would say that. Griffith claimed he'd just been keeping up appearances.

Switching tactics, prosecutor DiGiacomo asked Griffith

why he'd asked his roommate, Louis Colombo, to dismember Debbie's body and store it.

"Why would you ask your best friend to dismember a body if he had nothing to do with the killing?" DiGiacomo asked.

"Nobody wanted to be a part of anything like that," Griffith replied.

During the interviews with the police department, Griffith had also provided some contradictory information.

"As you sit here today, you can't remember if trying to lie your way out of this to the police happened before or after you dismembered the body?" the prosecution pressed.

"I said, in relation to the days, so many things were happening, so many different trips to the store, and this and that, that I don't remember what day was what in relation to the interview," Griffith said.

The jury went home for the weekend, and Judge Kathleen Delaney instructed them not to discuss the case with anybody. The cross-examination would continue on Monday.

Celeste was overjoyed at the prosecutor's cross-examination of Jason Griffith. She had been unusually silent on Facebook, perhaps understandably so, when Griffith had first taken the stand and answered his defense attorneys' questions. It was not lost on the older sister that Griffith was fighting for his life, and might get away with a verdict of manslaughter, but now she crowed:

"District Attorney started cross-examining today, and all I can say is BOOM! Got him stuttering and nervous as they are calling out lies left and right nonstop. Thanking God for the awesome job the DA is doing on representing my Lil Sister Debbie Flores-Narvaez. Their strategy is untouchable!"

On Monday, May 19, 2014, it was a new, defiant, annoyed, and visibly tired Jason Griffith who appeared for his fourth day of questioning at the courthouse. He even rolled his eyes as the prosecutor kept on asking him the same questions in a different way.

Wearing a royal blue shirt and a black suit, Griffith sat through hours of questioning, maintaining he'd been afraid of Debbie.

"Certainly by the time you had your arms around her, you had the upper hand, considering your size?" asked the prosecutor.

"The only thing I did was restrain her," Griffith insisted. "No banging, tossing, nothing like that, sir."

"You're telling the jury you held on to her long enough for her to die and you didn't realize you were in the process of asphyxiating her?"

"She's not gagging, not scratching. We fell backwards. I was talking to her," he said.

"Are you willing to acknowledge you did nothing to save the life of Debbie Flores?"

"I was in shock, sir."

"Are you willing to acknowledge not helping her?"

"I didn't do anything," Griffith replied.

"Thank you," DiGiacomo said, satisfied with Griffith's cold answer. The chief prosecutor had concluded his cross-examination.

The defense's final witness was Griffith's ex-girlfriend, Agnes Roux, a gorgeous woman in her midthirties with high cheekbones and auburn hair. Agnes was a dancer in another Cirque du Soleil extravaganza, and she testified that Debora Flores-Narvaez had been a violent woman who'd shown up everywhere the couple met to harass them. Agnes told the jurors how she'd witnessed Debbie push, slap, and spit on Jason Griffith. She recalled a time when Debbie showed up to the Mirage Hotel and Casino, waiting for her and Griffith in the parking lot.

"I've seen her spit on his face, and I've seen her slap him," Agnes said. "She was harassing us, and she was getting crazier and crazier."

Agnes testified that she had broken up with Griffith when she'd learned he was having an affair with Debbie, and that he was also sleeping with two other separate female fellow dancers from the Cirque du Soleil show *LOVE*. Before their breakup, Agnes had believed that she and Griffith had an exclusive and monogamous relationship. Now she would learn the truth.

Agnes also believed Griffith when he told her that Debbie was constantly stalking and harassing him. She was under the impression that his relationship with Debora had ended in May 2010. However, he continued to have sex with Debbie. Agnes Roux would slowly find out that Jason Griffith had lied to her, too.

Agnes described again how Debbie had pushed, slapped, and spit on Jason Griffith in the October 2010 incident while she yelled at him to tell Agnes the truth about their relationship. At one point, Debbie had begun to kick Griffith's car door and Griffith grabbed her by the shoulders to move her. Agnes said Debbie fell to the ground; Griffith didn't push her down. "Her fall seemed disproportionate" to how he'd grabbed her, Agnes recalled. Debbie then sat on the ground, crying, before Agnes helped her get up, she said.

Griffith was arrested and charged with coercion in the incident, but the case was later dropped. (Jason Griffith had appeared in court to testify as to the charges on December 22, 2010, but Debbie, of course, had not—since at that time, Debora had already been dead for more than a week.)

The jury also heard a recording of Agnes Roux calling 911 on Griffith's behalf after an incident where Debora was in her car, chasing Griffith to his home.

Agnes testified that in early December 2010, not long before Debbie's death, she and Jason Griffith had considered reconnecting, but said that she told Griffith she wouldn't get back together with him if he was still with Debbie and the two continued to have a sexual relationship.

"It was quite obvious she couldn't be in the picture if I was back," Agnes said.

So, according to prosecutor Michelle Fleck, Griffith took care of appearances.

Fleck later summed it up: "Debbie and Jason break up in June [2010]. Then Jason meets Agnes. Debbie slashes his car tires in June, and he films her admitting she did that. Finally, she walks away from him and wants nothing more to do with him, but on July 5th he texts her 'Happy Birthday.' And then they start a flirtation on the phone again. He asks her what she wants on her birthday. She talked about tennis shoes, and then he goes over to her place to give her money for the shoes and they have sex. And then, from July until October there are no incidents at all."

Once Jason meets Agnes, he apparently needs to find a cover for her with Debbie, according to prosecutor Michelle Fleck. "So on October 3 he calls 911 while Agnes is in the car with him." Fleck retraced the steps he took. "He says, 'What can I do about my [ex] girlfriend? She's harassing me.' The dispatcher asks him, 'When did this happen?' 'In June,' he says. And the dispatcher asks him, 'Why are you calling me now?' So, from June till the fall there are no problems. But then he calls 911 with Agnes in the car, to manipulate Agnes."

Testimony from some of Debbie's close friends has shown that their volatile relationship sparked into heated confrontation after Debbie Flores-Narvaez twice became pregnant and sought more attention from Griffith. He has said he became scared of her violent tendencies.

On cross-examination, prosecutor Michelle Fleck asked Agnes about the so-called threatening letter from Debbie that Griffith alleged to have found on his car, the letter that supposedly threatened Griffith with death if Debbie found him with another woman.

Fleck asked whether Agnes was aware that Griffith had learned four years ago that the note had actually been written by his roommate, Louis Colombo.

Agnes said she hadn't known that.

Fleck then asked Agnes to recall whether, after she had dumped him for cheating on her, Griffith had become suicidal.

Agnes remembered telling police she did not necessarily believe he was suicidal. "'I just believe he's a great actor,'" she said she told police, now with an ironic look on her face.

Although Griffith had previously testified that Agnes Roux was "the love of his life," now she did not even go visit him in jail.

"You're still in love with him. Is that correct?" Fleck asked.

"No," Agnes replied unequivocally.

"When you came in, you had a visible reaction to seeing him." Agnes's look at that point had been quizzical and almost sad, but ultimately inscrutable.

She replied that she hadn't seen Jason Griffith for years.

After Agnes Roux left the stand, the defense rested.

Before the trial, and before she was aware of Jason Griffith's avoidance of the truth on the stand, Agnes had written a letter in his support to Judge Kathleen Delaney. The letter is now public record and is reproduced here:

> *To the Judge or the Court,*
> *the Honorable Kathleen Delaney,*
>
> *Please find my letter of support to Jason Omar Griffith "Blu" to help you understand the good-hearted man he has been for many of us, outside the criminal justice system.*
>
> *I met Blu in May 2010, as he was the chosen choreographer for a charity event raising money for kids in the Las Vegas Community. This highly recognized fundraiser called "A Choreographer's showcase" is a sold out program happening once a year at the Mystere theatre (Treasure Island Hotel and*

Casino) It is a beautiful initiative born from the collaboration between world famous Cirque du Soleil and the Nevada Ballet Theatre.

Selected among other Cirque du Soleil artists volunteering their time and energy, Bluchoreographed a very moving dance piece for the high level athletes from Cirque du Soleil and the Nevda Ballet theatre dancers. It did represent about 3-4 months of work; of course, nobody was paid, it is simply a wonderful act of generosity than to put time and talent at the service of the Community.

Blu's ballet was the most memorable work that was presented. There was a spoken part in the music track, here again, his poetry stood out.

I saw him redirecting a rehearsal and I was amazed by the contract between his hip hop look and the extreme care and sensibility with which he was demonstrating to the male dancer how to hold his female partner. Gentle, he was teaching his dancers how to be very cautious, and he treated the lady as a very precious thing.

I was intrigued by this man dressed like a teenager but who seemed to havedepths of an accomplished artist. We exchanged numbers and started dating within 3 weeks.

I also work for Cirque du Soleil and all the connections I had in his show "LOVE" (Sandrine,

Mattei, Pendu, Eve Castello Blanco, Hassan, . . .
among others), spoke very highly about him: his flawless
work ethic, his perfect attendance, the fun reliable
colleague that he was, and the great friend they found
in him.

We had the same background. He is a trained
ballet and modern dancer; from a very reputable New
York School (La Guardia) I loved how wrong were my
first impressions of him.

His talent and creativity, with his commitment to
help the kids from the community through exposing
them to Art, Theatre, movement, or writing, were
quiet admirable for a young man at the epic of his
dance career.

I went to see him perform and his energy and
generosity on stage blew me away. Versatile, and
charismatic, he was interacting a lot with other
characters on stage; you could tell he was a great team
player.

He was bringing me a rose every single time
were meeting. It sounds cheesy, but I liked this
romantic side. He had been patient with me. I
respected that.

Just like me, he didn't smoke or drink. At all! I was
absolutely thrilled by that.

Interestingly enough, we never fought; he was this
very mature way to approach disagreement. Never was

he physically or orally abusive. I never saw him lose control or become disrespectful. He kept his voice down with me at all times.

I felt he was wise in relationship issues, he was even giving "couple counseling sessions" to his friends (Tina and Cameron, or Meredith and Brent for instance) they would call him and ask for his views and advices on their problems. They trusted his judgment. I was impressed by how he was able to take both sides into consideration and give a very fair recommendation on what should be done, or said, to fix the problem. I really felt that I was with a very special man.

With me he was very loving, supportive, tender and tolerant. Things were easy. He is very driven and ambitious, we both worked hard to meet our personal goal, but within the relationship, it was very peaceful.

Because of the high profile case with high media coverage he gets, I do not wish to testify in court, because of the impact it has on my personal life and my partner. I hope you will understand.

Nevertheless, I wish the Court should show Blu leniency for the generous citizen, loyal, talented dancer, and lovable man he is to us.

> *With all my due respect.*
> *Best regards.*
> *Agnes Roux.*

Agnes Roux, just like Debbie, had apparently been fooled by Jason Griffith's well-manufactured mask. I wondered what she thought of him now. But when I approached her after the trial, Agnes Roux declined to speak to me. She simply responded, "I'm sorry, Carolina. I can't."

Tuesday, May 20, 2014, the ninth day of trial, ended with an aggressive comeback from both sides. Jason Griffith, dressed in a white shirt and a black suit, paid close attention as both sides talked to the jurors, making their closing arguments before deliberations, walking the jury once more through all the testimonies they heard. It would be up to the jury now to decide whether Griffith was guilty of either first-degree murder, second-degree murder, or voluntary manslaughter—or whether he was not guilty of any of them and would be acquitted of all charges, a scenario that was now highly unlikely.

During more than three and a half hours of closing arguments, the defense asked the jury to consider Griffith's state of mind when he killed Debbie, telling the jury to consider another gender scenario: What if Jason Griffith was a woman and Debora Flores-Narvaez had been a man? What would have happened, and how would others react, if Griffith had been stalking and harassing Debbie, if he'd broken into her house, if he'd slashed the tires of her car, if he'd threatened her? Would she have had the right to defend herself?

Prosecutor Michelle Fleck, however, hammered home that Debora Flores-Narvaez "was a young woman, a successful woman, she loved her family, her friends, music, dancing, and in the end, she loved the wrong man."

DA Marc DiGiacomo put it even more bluntly. "Everything Mr. Griffith does is for Mr. Griffith," said the prosecutor, adding, "Debbie was nothing but a vehicle for his sexual appetite."

Jason Griffith had testified that he'd killed his ex-girlfriend, Debora Flores-Narvaez, in self-defense. The prosecutors questioned why Griffith said he thought Debbie was armed.

"Nobody on earth but Jason Griffith says she had a gun," DiGiacomo said.

Griffith looked annoyed at the proceedings. He could probably see which way the wind was blowing, and it was not in his favor.

"Tell the twelve people in the box the truth. That's all you had to do!" said DiGiacomo, practically shouting at Griffith and visibly frustrated. "Is there a single fact that he didn't lie to you about?" he again asked rhetorically of the jury.

Prosecutor Michelle Fleck argued, "If a 165-pound man takes his hands and wraps them around his girlfriend's throat, and compresses her throat to the point that she passes out and dies, there is absolutely no other reason that a man would do that if he was not trying to kill her."

Defense attorney Abel Yáñez countered that Debbie was volatile herself. "There were times when she was nice; there were times when she was sweet. But when she was violent, she would hit him, she would spit on him, she would slash his tires." Yáñez showed the jury the picture of Griffith's car with its flat tires.

Despite all efforts from the prosecutors to paint Jason as an aggressor, the defense's task was to convince the jury their client acted in self-defense.

THIRTEEN

◇◇◇

The Verdict

I had been following the case closely online, talking to my former colleagues and to Celeste every night after coming home from work in Los Angeles, California.

After nine days of arguments and almost two days of deliberation, the jury of seven men and five women finally reached a verdict on May 22, 2014: guilty of second-degree murder. After first-degree murder, this was the harshest sentence that could be handed down. Once the verdict was read, the jury went out through the back door, so no reporters were able to ask them any questions.

Jason Griffith sat motionless as the verdict was read, and only blew a kiss to his mother, Charlene Davis. His attorney Abel Yáñez placed one arm around his shoulders.

Debbie Flores-Narvaez's family cried and hugged one

another while hearing it. Although it was not as hefty a sentence as she'd hoped, Celeste had been waiting to hear the word "guilty" for almost four years.

After the trial ended, media reporters surrounded the prosecutors and the families.

Marc DiGiacomo, the DA, said they understood why the jury had gone for second-degree murder, and that they "respected the jury's verdict."

"There's no question this was a domestic dispute. But whenever there is a question of premeditated, if a jury can't agree on first-degree murder or second-degree murder the jury is instructed to then come back with a second-degree murder verdict," DiGiacomo said. "We certainly respect that decision."

"Everyone thought this would be a death penalty case, and it's satisfying that we got a verdict of second-degree murder," said defense lawyer Abel Yáñez, adding that his client still had several issues to appeal on, such as the various pieces of evidence the judge had not allowed shown in the trial, items that they felt would've shown more of Debbie's violent behavior toward Jason Griffith. "As to the verdict, in general I think it was a fair one based on the evidence the jury was allowed to hear. There were several legal rulings by the judge that prevented critical evidence from being presented to the jury. For example, the secret video taken by Jason of Debbie Flores-Narvaez admitting to all her crimes, stalking, and harassing was not seen by the jury."

The attorney was referring to the video where Debbie admits slashing Jason's car tires and throwing egg whites on it, as well as looking in his computer and slapping him.

Judge Kathleen Delaney had ruled out that particular video, which the defense had considered "critical for the jury to see, as it not only corroborated Jason's story, but it gave an example of Debbie's violent character and demeanor. The several jurors I spoke to afterwards asked about the video and how they wanted to see it."

"We had hoped to represent a clearer picture of the relationship, which was even stormier than what the jury was allowed to hear," Yáñez said. "Nevertheless, I was still hoping for a manslaughter verdict even with the evidence that was excluded by the judge."

Yáñez said Griffith was disappointed with the verdict and felt that the jury would have reached a different result if the jury members had gotten all the facts and evidence.

"Sometimes I have to remind myself, 'Abel, at the end of the day, it is not you who will be sleeping in jail,'" he told me later. He says he starts to "suffer" when he sees his client on the stand making a mistake, or saying something he knows will cost his client a longer sentence or worse conviction.

Also speaking for the defense, attorney Jeff Banks

added, "That's trial work. Truth at trial is always seen by a jury through the goggles of evidentiary admissibility."

Debbie's mother, Elsie Narvaez, said in Spanish: "We plan to come back as many times as he tries to appeal. We won't allow him to." Now her tears had given way to anger. "When someone kills once, they lose their fear of God, and they'll do it again."

Debbie's father, Carlos Flores, a laconic and private man with a dry sense of humor, said of Jason Griffith's tears while on the stand: "His tears didn't even coincide with his emotions. He is going to be dancing; the only difference is that he's going to be dancing to a different tune now and he's going to remember her name for the rest of his life." Carlos Flores has declined to speak with the authors for this book.

On the other side, Charlene Davis declined to speak to anyone. "I don't want to talk right now. I have to talk to my son's attorneys," she said.

Defense attorney Yáñez said he advised his client not to speak to anyone at all about the case until all of his appeals were exhausted. He stated that they would appeal: "In Nevada, a defendant has thirty days from the filing of the judgment of conviction to file his notice of appeal, which we will do."

Then came Marc DiGiacomo, the aggressive prosecutor. Had it been his strategy going in to prove that Jason Griffith was a liar and a narcissist?

"Well, yes," he said with a small laugh. "It was pretty clear to me Mr. Griffith didn't have any empathy for anybody except himself." Recalling the note on Griffith's car, which Griffith attributed to Debbie but the prosecutor proved he'd actually known all along was only a bad joke from his roommate, DiGiacomo said, "After the first ten minutes I knew that I had him."

"I don't know how he couldn't have known about that writing on his car," DiGiacomo said. "He requested we show the video of Debbie being 'violent,' and it was in there, on that disc." DiGiacomo referred to the disc of information obtained from Jason Griffith's computer—the disc had included not only the video of Debbie, but backups of all Griffith's text messages. "But this guy had so many text messages from so many girls! And I came across that writing the night before. I thought, 'Oh my God that was fun!'" The prosecutor relished having caught Jason in one of his biggest lies yet. "That was the plan on cross-examination. It didn't [even] look like Debbie's handwriting. When I came across the writing it was like 'Oh boy!'"

Although he understood why Celeste, Debbie's sister, had wanted a harsher verdict—"I understand Celeste wanted more. She's been very active from the very beginning," and as prosecutor Michelle Fleck said, "she makes you wish if anything happened to you, that there would be someone around who is a crusader for justice, like she is"—the DA said he hadn't expected to get a verdict of capital murder. "We knew we didn't have the kind of case for death penalty at all. We chose as an office not to pursue a death penalty sentence. We didn't feel a man in his thirties with no previous criminal record [would get that verdict]. We felt the jury would come back with second." Although Griffith had accusations of domestic violence against him, and had been briefly incarcerated for this offense, he had not committed murder before.

Were the prosecutors satisfied with the verdict? "Well, I believe the judge will give him life in prison," DiGiacomo said. "He will be a very old man before he gets out of jail."

It would be two more months before anyone would know if the prosecutor's theory was correct. The sentencing would be handed down on July 23, 2014, at 9:30 A.M., about two weeks after what would have been Debbie's thirty-fifth birthday.

During the trial, Celeste said the courtroom was full of not only reporters, dancers, and Debbie's friends but also a lot of people who had read about the case and felt, like I did, that they knew Debbie. Celeste was very thankful for all the support. I spoke to her briefly, and she said she was exhausted, but that the verdict closed an important chapter in their lives. "I don't want anyone else to ever go through the pain I've been and I'm still going through."

But even Jason Griffith's conviction was not enough for Celeste to find peace and closure.

On May 31, 2014, about nine days after the verdict, Celeste posted on Facebook:

"I know I haven't spoken since the trial and Las Vegas. A lot of friends and loved ones are asking or want to make sure how I'm doing and don't get a response I'm sorry about that. Truth is, I'm not sure about any of it at this point or the verdict. It hurts a lot. I'm shutting myself off and away from everyone and family. I know it's not good. But I'm stubborn and I feel alone in a bubble."

Would she ever forgive Jason?

"No," she said later. "Although, I've learned to forgive others for me, I could never forgive him."

The trial had been "especially hard for *mami*," Celeste said. They hadn't been expecting to see photos of Debbie's autopsy in court, and when they were shown, "I just had to cover my mom's eyes."

But despite being highly upset, Celeste had managed to remain composed in the courtroom. The first time she had appeared in court, she'd had an outburst, shouting expletives at Griffith, and she'd had to be removed.

"I just had to control myself in the courtroom. I did it for Mom," she said.

Celeste posted links to the verdict along with photos

of her sister on Facebook. Finally, she made her feelings clear:

"Why Second Degree Murder was given for my little Sister Debbie's murderer? I'm still speechless about it all. Call it shock. It hasn't hit me yet, but at least this question was answered."

Celeste was referring to an interview with one of the jurors, Vincent King, who had tried to clarify how the jurors, who had deliberated for two days, had finally settled on the second-degree verdict, even though prosecutors and Celeste wanted to hear first degree.

King said it was a difficult verdict. He was aware that neither the victim's family nor the prosecutors would be happy with the second-degree murder verdict, and admitted that, at first, he, too, had been in favor of Murder One, but said he'd wavered between second- and first-degree murder when Jason Griffith was cross-examined. Griffith had certainly not helped his cause any. Vincent King said he thought Griffith had seemed arrogant and unremorseful.

But the juror explained that, according to instructions, the jury had had to determine whether the murder was premeditated, and they came to the conclusion that it was not. King said he felt confident that they made the right decision.

FOURTEEN

◇◇◇

Reactions

The reaction of the Las Vegas community to the trial verdict seemed to be a general consensus of total outrage over Jason Griffith's actions. After his arrest in January 2011, most of the cast members of both *FANTASY* and *LOVE* had turned their backs on him. Most of them said he was a monster, and they sided with Debbie.

Rene Delgadillo, the magician with whom Debbie worked on occasion, was of that mind-set: "Well, I am very disappointed to say the least," he said of the verdict. "I'm just not too happy about the way it all turned out for Debbie. There was no justice at all." Rene, like Celeste, still wanted Jason Griffith to receive a life in prison without parole sentence, if it could not be the death penalty.

But not everyone was surprised by the verdict. Luke

Ciciliano, the attorney and personal friend of Debbie's who'd represented her in her lawsuit against Jamile McGee, said that "the trial went about as I expected it to and I can't say that there were really any surprises.

"I guess being a lawyer gave me a little different perspective. I think I would have to say that my main reaction to the decision is a sense of relief that Debbie's family can potentially have closure to this aspect of the situation; while it will never be 'behind them' they can stop worrying about this part of the process and, hopefully, they can start worrying about the 'healing' process instead of what's going on with the court situation."

He hoped that the verdict would help bring closure to the family, though he was of the opinion that "finding that closure is up to the family now. I personally have never believed in the end result of a criminal case bringing closure to a family. There's lots of research that shows that a verdict has little to do with how a victim's loved ones deal with things going forward."

Ciciliano said he believed Debbie herself would also have focused on her family's well-being, and less on the results of the trial. "I think the bigger focus on how Debbie would have felt would have been concern for her loved ones going forward and not so much on the case itself."

Sonya Sonnenberg, Debbie's roommate and the person who'd called in a missing person's report on her to police, said she'd had "a bad feeling" when Debbie disappeared.

The roommate stated that when Debbie first went missing, she'd assumed Jason Griffith had her. "But I didn't think that he had killed her," at least not at first. "After days went by, I kind of assumed that she was dead, but you never know. We didn't want to make any assumptions."

Sonya, who is cool and logical, also stated that she believed the verdict was the right one, though she, too, hoped for a stiff sentence. "I think it was correct, because in order to be first-degree murder it had to be premeditated, but I hope that he gets more than ten years because of everything he did afterwards. There were aggravating circumstances, and it makes my skin crawl, what he did to her afterwards, that somebody could do that to someone else, especially someone they claimed to love at some point."

#JusticeForDebbie was a social media hashtag created by Debbie's friends and family members during her trial. Just like the news outlets covered Debbie's murder trial, in social media, everyone in the dancing community was getting their information, and most were using #Justice ForDebbie whenever they referred to the case.

Social media had been very active—Celeste in particular on Facebook—but some people chose to stay away.

Mia Guerrero, the first person who'd reached out to me when she'd heard that her good friend was missing, said she'd tried to stay away from the trial and the gossip. To her, Debbie was and will always be in her heart.

Mia had been very close to Debbie, and the passing of the Puerto Rican beauty who'd made her laugh left an empty space in her fellow dancer's life, though Mia said she knew that time went on.

Mia, a wife and mother of two, was now focused on her family. Even though she didn't go to the trial, it was all over the news, and she'd heard bits and pieces about it. She knew that Jason Griffith had been found guilty, but she hadn't wanted to know any more than that.

Last time we spoke, Griffith had been awaiting his sentence, but as far as she was concerned, his fate was in God's hands, and she preferred to leave it at that.

The same could be said of Marci Gee, one of Griffith's ex-girlfriends, now twenty-seven years old. She had since changed jobs and was in a very stable relationship with a new boyfriend.

But Marci had some poignant and revealing thoughts about her past relationship with Jason Griffith.

"It could have been me," was her opener, and then she continued with a wise musing: "We never do think bad things could happen to us. We do not expect them, and we think, 'That would never happen to me.'"

She said she now thinks about the episode almost every day. "The trial, everything that came out of it was very shocking and painful," Marci said. "It was painful because of the fact that he lied to my face so many times." Ever since Debbie's disappearance, there has not been a day when she doesn't tell herself, "I could have been Debbie. I could be dead now."

Only a month before Debbie was brutally murdered and dismembered, Marci had been considering getting back together with Jason.

In September 2010, Marci had moved to San Diego, California, for a month. During that period, Griffith had called her, texted her, looked for her, and tried to convince her to come back to him, that she was the only woman in his life.

"I am not sure if you could call what we had a formal relationship," she said, qualifying that the two would date "on and off." "I remember asking all my girlfriends. I would ask them if I should believe he was single and committed to me."

No one could give her an answer, but deep inside, Marci had a feeling it was not true. She knew he was a player.

"I was so tempted to go to his house, but now, I am so relieved I never did. I could have been Debbie. It could have been me," she repeated.

By this point, it had been almost four years since Marci had last seen Jason in person, though she clearly remembers the last time they hung out, at his house.

She was surprised that Louis Colombo had testified in court against Griffith, especially because the two men were so close. Marci remembered when Griffith had lived in a converted garage in the same house as Louis and his wife, before the couple split up, so she'd heard.

Griffith had told her that his roommate was an unconditional friend. He referred to him as a "brother," and said that when Griffith was having difficult economic times, Louis helped him with his expenses.

"It seemed like a good friendship. I could not believe that Louis and Agnes appeared in court to testify against him," Marci remarked, still surprised. She had known about Griffith's relationship with the dancer Agnes Roux.

All her friends knew that Marci had been dating Jason Griffith for a while, so when the trial finally started, and the TV stations began to cover the story and make headlines on local and national television, Marci had no other option but to hear what was going on.

When her mother found out that Marci had been dating the guy now in the news facing murder charges, she was very worried. After all, this was a case that issued a warning to all women, like the neon lights that illuminate most of Las Vegas. If you're in relationship that turbulent, RUN. Do not become another Debbie.

Marci, like the majority of people, was unsurprised when Griffith was found guilty, and she hoped that he would spend many years in jail for what he did. Not because she wanted to punish him, she said, but because she felt he needed time to fully comprehend the extent of his actions toward women. "I think it's better for him to stay in jail. For his own good. I am not sure what could happen to him if he gets out of jail now or so soon."

No woman, no human being deserves to die like Debbie did, but Marci thought Debbie should have known better. "What do I think about Debbie? For Jason, I feel pity. In Debbie's case, I feel she could have prevented this."

Marci also mentioned that Jason Griffith had gone to jail once before, which kind of raised a red flag for her. He told her his ex-wife had been cheating on him and when he'd found out who she was "fooling around with," he'd confronted the guy and assaulted him so badly that Griffith ended up in jail.

"If Jason was violent once, he could become violent again and he did. I could have been Debbie and this is very scary." She repeated her mantra.

"What did I learn from this? Not to ever date a man I find on the Internet," she said with a soft, bitter laugh.

FIFTEEN

◇◇◇

Domestic Violence

Throughout this whole case, a major question to my mind and to the minds of many others had always been, how and why had Debbie let herself get into these violent situations over and over again? She was a smart, beautiful, talented woman with multiple advanced degrees, and she'd found success in the difficult entertainment business. So why had she been drawn to men with whom she had such volatile relationships?

Looking for answers, I turned to Rebeca Ferreira, a delightful, charismatic woman in her forties from the Dominican Republic. Rebeca is now the director and founder of Safe Faith United, a nonprofit organization that started with an almost homeless woman wanting to make a difference in her community, wanting other women not to go through her same experiences: domestic violence.

Everyone who works as a journalist in Las Vegas knows Rebeca. Fortunately for us, she is often our main contact in the most odd, tragic, and unique stories. Unfortunately for the victims, most of them never get to meet this remarkable woman in person.

Debbie Flores-Narvaez's picture hangs outside Rebeca's office, where she has a gallery of photos, some of them very disturbing and graphic, of women who have been killed by their partners. I met Rebeca when I first arrived to work in Sin City. She was helping out a twenty-one-year-old, undocumented young woman from Mexico in a very abusive relationship, so much her boyfriend would close the door of their little apartment leaving the girl and their son to sleep outside in the hallway. The boyfriend ended up kidnapping their son, and without her permission, of course, took him out of the country.

This was a very long process, but thanks to many national and local stories, and with the help of different organizations in both countries, Rebeca and I were able to bring the child back to the United States, and the woman was able to apply for a humanitarian visa. Our efforts were such that we were recognized with one of the most prestigious journalistic awards, an Emmy, for the best crime coverage.

Rebeca is one of the most courageous women I have

met in my career. To place it in perspective as to how passionate this woman is with her victims, when I first met Rebeca, she didn't even have enough money to put gas in her car to go see a victim. She had to do it based on donations. Now, almost seven years later, she has become a voice for all those women who maintain silence on their abusive relationships. She is so dedicated because she was part of the statistics.

Rebeca used to work for the North Las Vegas Police Department as an interpreter. Ironically, while she was herself a silent victim of domestic violence, she was mostly called upon to translate for women who had contacted the police after domestic disputes.

Rebeca, like most of the victims of domestic violence, was also embarrassed to tell her family and, even more so, the police department what was going on at home. But one day, when her sister came to visit from Canada, Rebeca decided to open her heart and confess what was going on: that her husband had been abusing her for years. After talking to her sister, Rebeca decided to leave her husband and find a path to save her own life and the lives of others.

Every time Rebeca Ferreira hears about a domestic violence case, her own memories of being abused come back to life. She remembers how it feels to be put down time and again, and to feel the need to be silent, to feel embarrassed, or to even feel guilty. This happened to

Debbie as well, feeling minimized by her lover, like she meant nothing to him and he had to keep dalliances with other women.

The numbers fluctuate, but a study released by the Violence Policy Center in 2012 revealed that Nevada's rate of women killed by men was the highest in the nation. During that same year, Las Vegas police handled more than twenty-two thousand domestic violence–related cases where a crime was committed—and the authorities responded to more than *sixty thousand* calls for domestic-related cases in the course of a single year.

In 2010, the year Debora was killed, Nevada also had the highest percentage of murders related to domestic violence. Sadly, Debbie became one more number to add to this very tragic statistic.

I wanted to know why there were so many instances of domestic violence and violence against women in Las Vegas in particular. Why Las Vegas?

"Some say the drinks, the drugs, the casinos, the strip clubs, but to me, they're all excuses." Rebeca has seen the most horrifying cases in Las Vegas in particular, but she emphasized that men and women, not only in Nevada, but all over the world, need to have faith. Whatever it is you believe in, she says, the lack of faith from both sides is, to her, the main reason why we see so much violence. The day she devoted her life to God, she believed and understood she deserved better, and she stopped the cycle of domestic violence.

As a woman, it is terrifying to read and to report these cases. The statistics from the National Coalition Against Domestic Violence are alarming:

- 3 to 4 million American women are battered each year, yet battery is the most under-reported crime in America.

- 95% of all spouse abuse cases are women who are hurt by men.

- Battering occurs among people of all races.

- A battering incident is rarely an isolated event, and tends to increase and become more violent over time.

A couple of days before I'd reached out to her to talk about Debbie, Rebeca had helped the family of a woman whose husband beat her to death with a belt. Her husband had been upset because she'd gambled away almost all of her paycheck at a local casino.

"There must never be a reason why a woman has to become a victim of assault," Rebeca observed. "Just like Debbie. Jason claimed she was a stalker, but yet, he continued the relationship with her, and ended her life."

"Debbie's murder is one of the most brutal cases I've seen. One was a woman whose hands were cut off with a machete; the other, a woman stabbed more than 150 times, and now Debbie. None of them had a peaceful death," said Rebeca. "Debbie was a dancer, a performer; her body was her instrument for work. Jason committed the most humiliating act on her: he chopped her legs off!" Rebeca noted, almost crying.

Many people I'd talked to had said the same thing, that "Debbie liked bad boys." But Rebeca became upset every time she heard someone say such a thing.

"No woman is crazy enough to like a 'bad boy; no woman likes to be abused. This is a lie. We fall in love with a good man, but then this man shows his true colors and we love him so much, we hope he changes, and he never does. If we wait too long, we could end up dead like Debora," she told me in a very agitated tone. And yes, Debbie had hoped that she could change Jason Griffith. "Respect me," she pleaded with him at one point according to one of her friends, Merriliz Monzon.

Annette Scott is the outreach program manager in Las Vegas for S.A.F.E. House, which stands for Stopping Abuse in the Family Environment. She is proud to say she has been an advocate for victims for seventeen years, first with victims of crime and then for domestic violence.

"There is nothing to 'get'!" Annette states about Debbie's friends and family members who didn't understand her loyalty to Jason Griffith, especially considering what an intelligent, strong, independent woman Debora Flores-Narvaez was.

"It's not unusual for people to find unhealthy relationships over and over again, regardless of their status in life or their educational background," said Annette.

As to Debbie's previous domestic violence incident with Jamile McGee, Annette is of the same mind-set: "We're not going to have a concrete answer as to why she was in another domestic violence incident. There are women who are involved; not only are the men manipulative but they are predators. You can have a hundred university degrees but that's not going to protect you."

"Some people question, 'Why did she go back there?'" Annette said of Debbie, who kept going back to Jason Griffith. "None of us has the right to judge her. He was out to hurt her. He may have been threatening her. This is a man who went as far as to manipulate her, and yet some people will report that she was violent. I remember seeing an argument online about her stalking him. The whole thing doesn't make any sense." No matter what, he had an option to stop.

And then the advocate adds, sadly and sardonically: "He had two domestic violence charges, so was it easier for him to kill her and mutilate her? That sounds to me more like the MO of a serial killer! My concern is, where is the history of violence in his background?"

Annette expounded on what she believed was Jason Griffith's character.

"We have an extreme narcissistic personality; mutilating a human being was nothing to him. To have no remorse and say he was doing it to protect himself, we have someone who was really sick. Even if she had stalked him, he is a sick, sick man. The reality of domestic violence is that it crosses all lines. . . . They are the worst kind of predator there is. I'm not surprised more did not come out in the court. A lot of times prosecutors don't focus on the history of violence because this is a murder case." That was true: prosecutors are not legally allowed to bring up a defendant's previous history; they may only focus on the case at hand.

But Jason Griffith's ex-wife had told Dr. Phil's production team that he had punched her in the face, which the host mentioned during the broadcast, and that makes Annette Scott see red: "A wife stating that, this man is just sicker than how they tried to portray him. There had to be warning signs about him," she said. Nor did she believe Jason Griffith's verdict was fair: "No, I don't think he should have gotten second degree, no. I know there has to be an amount of premeditation. [. . .] Remember, manipulation is the key to a personality disorder. Her sister and her family will play the most important role at the parole hearings. They have to make sure that the perpetrator does not go unpunished."

In Annette's more general estimation, "Women should try to get away from men who try to hurt them and eventually kill them. We have an epidemic, not only in our country, but all over the world."

Despite all the unofficial diagnoses of Jason being "a narcissist," however, that still did not explain all of his behavior—or Debbie's.

Olga E. Hervis, MSW (master of social work), LCSW (licensed clinical social worker), is the coauthor and codeveloper of *Brief Strategic Family Therapy (BSFT) and Family Effectiveness Therapy (FET),* a nationally recognized and award-winning book.

In 2003, she founded the Family Therapy Training Institute of Miami in order to disseminate her thirty-five years of education, research, and practice in this field.

The therapist believed that Debbie suffered from what is called "dependent personality disorder," and that Jason Griffith preyed on that. "Predators can smell sick, injured, lost prey. I am convinced that these predatory individuals have a sixth sense to uncover women like her."

Dr. Hervis offered an appropriate allegory from a comic strip, no less:

"Remember the old Charlie Brown cartoon where Lucy holds the football and promises Charlie she will not move it this next time?" the therapist says with a knowing laugh. "Charlie, who actually knows better from all the past experiences, still decides he needs to give her one more chance and trust her. Of course, Lucy removes the ball as he is kicking it, and Charlie falls and bumps his head on the ground. This, my friend, is the nature of these repetitive abusive patterns. The abuser knows it and almost every single time engages in what psychology calls [in Behavior Conditioning Theory], an 'Alternating-Opposing Reinforcement program.'

"It goes like this: The rat is taught to navigate a maze and gets rewarded with food at the end, until she has learned it. After that, in an alternating fashion, the rat runs the maze, gets food, runs the maze, and the rat gets an electric shock. Over and over and the rat never remembers the shock, just the food, so she keeps doing it as long as you want to run the experiment. These men alternate love and roses and 'I'm sorrys' with abuse. The victim becomes a rat. A friend of mine, years ago, gave me a great T-shirt. It read: 'Neurotics build castles in the air, Psychotics live in them, Personality disorders refuse to believe they are not there.'"

Then Dr. Hervis moved on to her diagnosis of Jason Griffith: "Narcissistic, abusive men view women as objects, not people. He is not necessarily psychotic, but more likely psychopathic, with no conscience."

As to the manner of death and the way he amputated Debbie's legs, she observed: "It is like cutting up a piece of furniture and disposing of it for *his* convenience. He had no regard for his victim as he does not see her as human like him. The world of narcissists revolves entirely around them and is *only* about them."

The therapist noted that she wasn't enough of a legal expert to weigh in on the verdict, but in her opinion, she hoped he would never get out of jail, "because undoubtedly he will continue to abuse and probably kill again the next time a woman becomes inconvenient or a nuisance."

There remained yet another psychological hurdle: If Debbie had been presumably stalking and harassing Jason Griffith, why did he stay in touch? Why did he seek her out on Facebook? Why did he let her in his home at all on that fateful night? And then, being considerably stronger than her—obviously strong enough to strangle and dismember her—why didn't he instead simply drag her, kicking and screaming, out of his house?

The most likely answer was anger, and yes, a "heat of the moment" decision, as he'd told investigators, to be rid of this annoying ex-lover for whom he no longer cared. But he'd certainly had time to change his mind: before he'd placed the plastic bag over her head; before he'd strangled her; and particularly before he'd decided to conceal her body by amputating her legs and sticking her, like something disposable, inside a storage bin.

SIXTEEN

◇◇◇

Psychological Evaluation

I found it difficult to figure out just what Jason Griffith's appeal was to women. It lies in a combination of bad boy good looks and a little-boy-lost quality, which he apparently used relentlessly and with total impunity. Examining his behavior during and after the murder, a picture emerges of a complete sociopath. He felt entitled to do what he did, to Debbie and to the other women to whom he had lied repeatedly. Jason Griffith was beholden to no one but Jason Griffith. He was the lead in his dances, the vortex of his own solipsistic universe. He was not to be held accountable for killing Debbie and concealing her body. She had brought it upon herself: he killed her because she stalked him; he hid her body because it smelled;

He was simply not guilty of anything, according to Jason Griffith.

Still seeking answers to why Debora Flores-Narvaez and Jason Griffith's stormy relationship ended so tragically, I contacted Dr. Luis Gaviria, one of the most respected clinical psychologists I've met in my career, in the hopes that he could help me analyze their behavior. Dr. Gaviria is not a forensic psychologist, but he is a neurobiological psychologist, and I trust his judgment, both as a psychologist and as a human being.

"Taking into consideration the many details from this case, I will give you my opinion from the position of a member of society, a fellow human being. I am a husband, a father, and a grandfather. I am also a son and a brother. I happen to know about human nature because I have training in psychotherapy and neuroscience, because I am a member of a neurosurgery team, because I have dealt with human pain for many years, but most of it all because I am a human being with a fair deal of life training."

He said it was difficult to make sense of such a senseless situation, but he wanted people to learn from it and avoid the kind of pain that is brought when we allow ourselves to act as Jason did.

Everybody, Dr. Gaviria explained to me, has two natural tendencies: searching for reward and pulling away from fear and pain.

However, he said, "When someone is seeking pain, something is not right.

"From the very perspective of love, there was very little of that. We see a relationship marked by lies, sex, betrayal, and struggle." But when a good sex experience becomes mixed with feelings of anger and violence and continuous fighting, our brain starts to associate those experiences, creating a very powerful addictive mix, he explained.

"This is the kind of topic that people tend to avoid. Many couples resolve their fights with sex, and this is trouble for any relationship. It is a very strong recipe for disaster. They kept on having sex because that was probably all they had left."

In a healthy relationship, as a couple, people should have tenderness, comfortable silence, the experience of being validated and admired, and sharing simple things besides sex itself.

He said that just the very fact that Griffith was still entangled in this troubled relationship showed that he had emotional issues, and so did Debbie.

"This was an interactive mess."

Going back to the final argument between Debbie and Jason, he explained it was understandable that Jason wanted to make her stop screaming, fighting, slapping him (if that was the true scenario that night), but in this case, he'd used extreme prejudice. He'd found the time and the articulation of actions to go and look for a bag and put it on her head and asphyxiated her, was Dr. Gaviria's assessment. If this was a "heat of the moment" type of case, he could have made different choices.

"The first thing that arises from the facts that we know is that this guy had a choice," the doctor affirmed. "He was not a Jack of the Street; he was very agile, a highly trained athlete with plenty of ability to control the situation physically, protect himself without having to kill her."

Dr. Gaviria knows all the facts presented in court. If Jason Griffith had come to him as a therapy client, he would've considered him someone who needed to learn how to manage his anger and frustration. He believed that frustration and anger piled up and accumulated.

"Sometimes we react from the very primitive part of our brain, and in this case, his anger triggered the worst of reactions. Unless he's prone to violence, he would have chosen another way of acting. Anyone can be bugged, slapped, annoyed, screamed at, but not everyone is going to react [by] killing someone." Furthermore, "I don't think any mentally healthy human being would be able to carry out all that plan without remorse and disgust. The very fact that he could look at the [autopsy] pictures in public [during the trial] without showing any emotion or remorse shows someone who exhibits psychotic traits."

After learning about such a gruesome account, one of the things Dr. Gaviria could choose as a take away is to consider the immense danger of engaging in stormy relationships that lead only to pain, an empty life, and possibly a tragedy. In his experience with clients throughout the past thirty years, he says life gravitates around two powerful sources, love and fear.

"Everything that spins from love, invites to tenderness, caring and soothing, companionship, forgiveness, and the construction of a meaningful life. Everything that spins from fear, besides our basic survival instincts and self-preservation, when justified, brings anger, frustration, helplessness, and sometimes chaotic actions."

Jason was moved by both fear and anger, Dr. Gaviria explained. He was afraid of losing his position at Cirque du Soleil, of going to jail, of losing the appreciation of his other girlfriends. Trying to escape from the consequences of his anger, his fears came true.

"He was someone so physically gifted who became the dancer of one of the best entertainment shows in the world, he had everything going for him. He was someone who worked for the *LOVE* show that was ironically searching for love in the wrong way."

And Debbie was also looking for love, but in the wrong place and with the wrong person?

"Yes, we see a beautiful young woman, talented, great dancer, someone who holds a master's degree, and someone who is evidently bound for success; a young lady who leaves a career searching for meaning in her life. She was looking for recognition, for meaning that [she] probably didn't find in her former life."

Jason, too, was in love—but with himself, Dr. Gaviria pointed out.

"When we look at Mr. Griffith's behavior, he seems to exhibit some narcissistic traits. Narcissists are extremely sensitive to criticism. They can't take feedback, but they can criticize other people to a dangerous extreme. If they don't see themselves as superior, they feel worthless. They usually have a dismissive attitude towards other people's needs. They don't care for other people. They are very competitive and tend to be envious."

We observed this as Jason and Debbie played a video game during the video of "Sex Games" and Debbie won and Jason dismissed her win like it was nothing.

Narcissists, Dr. Gaviria explains, are not driven by values of morals; they are driven by the fear of punishment. They would refrain from hurting someone not out of empathy or concern for the well-being of the other person, but out of fear of punishment.

"They are very external people, and they tend to be dishonest and cruel."

According to Dr. Gaviria, Jason Griffith was addicted— he needed the thrill, his fix, his dose, of good sex and physical satisfaction to get by, like other people might feel compelled to smoke cigarettes or have drinks.

"They feel like they are entitled to everything; they hate to live alone."

How about Debbie?

"After looking and analyzing her behavior, she was possessive, intense, and passionate in nature. It seems she could never find someone who could fulfill the desires of her soul. She was looking for love. Looking at his profile, I wouldn't be surprised, if he would put her down time and again. This beautiful girl [also] became addicted to the thrill of good sex and emotional strife."

The psychologist points out that some people feel alive only when they are angry or sexually excited. Debbie wanted to feel alive, looking for love, and got entangled in this "let's try again, let's have sex." She was saying, "love me, love me."

"She was not [really] looking for sex, she was looking for love and it seems like she never got it."

Dr. Gaviria made it clear that in spite of what anyone might have expressed in their interviews, we might never understand what really happened in detail, nor are we capable of judging the facts or the people involved.

But, Dr. Gaviria continued, "We all need emotional closure. Without it, there is this unbearable void in our chest, a wound that never heals. That's why kidnapping could become even more painful than murder itself. Only when we see a dead body or utter evidence that a loved one is dead, we can begin to mourn properly and eventually get closure. In time, pain will subside or at least diminish and we can go back to a functional life."

He said to remember that through neuroscience we learn that we are neurobiologically "programmed for justice." He explained, "That's why we enjoy movies with a just end: when the bad guys get what they deserve, we all experience a sense of closure and satisfaction. There is this feeling of retribution, that not properly managed could lead to relentless revenge, and possibly create a cascade of unfortunate happenings that end up turning victims into perpetrators, like when we take justice in our own hands. In our souls there is this notion: wrongdoers should be subject to the same pain and suffering they caused in the first place. Justice is embedded in our system. From our hearts and minds, justice should always be served."

He later added, "Justice is, from the point of view of neuroscience, wired into our nervous system, in our brain. It's part of us at a very biological level to be deeply touched and yearning for balance. Justice, when served, brings a sense of relief for those hurting. This is not a whim of the moment or the reaction of a petty heart. That's why we understand the reactions of Debora's family members. [. . .] I have born witness to the long-term effects of pain inflicted upon individuals and groups. People can be hurt so much, that their day-to-day routines get totally impaired. Some can't simply concentrate, without being able to carry out simple tasks, let alone keep a job and make a living.

"There is also an unbearable void in the chest and solar plexus, that makes it hard to even breathe. The obsessive thinking around the lost loved ones, the longing for their presence, the images related to their demise, all lead to extremely high levels of stress that limits the capacity to feel love and experience hope and peace.

"Trusting again, building meaningful relationships can also be very difficult for someone undergoing such circumstances. This is when psychotherapy, provided by highly trained therapists, can bring relief and healing. Thinking that time alone will take care of pain is a myth. Seeking professional help is imperative," he said, though he also noted that "properly guided support groups also do a lot for people that have suffered traumatic losses. Prayer does work for believers."

Dr. Gaviria also focused on the path to healing and the uselessness of self-blame. "One thing that is absolutely necessary to start a proper healing process is to get rid of the blame that loved ones cast upon themselves. I am talking about considerations like 'what did I do wrong? What didn't I give to my child that lead her/him to make such choices?' This holds true for the family of the victims and also for the perpetrators. Let's remember that we all have free will, and no matter how loving and supportive a family can be, children get to choose, especially the people they hang out with. That in itself can be a potent influence in the way we get to see life and love." On the other hand, he did not dismiss what he called "slight biological 'errors' that arise in the way DNA is passed on to descendants." He said, "Little malformations in the brain can lead people to react in not so adequate ways that lead to bad outcomes." In those cases, he said, parents "must take charge of our own choices, the ways we raise our children, and try to make up for our mistakes when possible, people choose to act in ways that bring tragedy."

Ultimately, Dr. Gaviria said, he wished for all who suffered to find relief. "I wish, deep in my heart, that those in pain will start to experience a sense of relief, and winds of hope. There is another wish in me, that we all learn from this tragedy. That we all become more aware of the quality of our relationships, that we remember the fact that we are here on this Earth to care for each other, that today being yet another day, being with our loved ones is a precious gift.

"I hope that we all learn something from this moving story."

SEVENTEEN

✧✧✧

Debbie Lives On . . .

"Help needed in search for missing Las Vegas woman."

This was the first post ever published on the Facebook page created for Debora Flores-Narvaez by her family and friends who, at the time, did not know that she was already dead. It was created in the hope that she would be found and returned to her family. That was when Celeste first went to Las Vegas looking for her sister.

By the time this page went public, Jason Griffith and Louis Colombo had already dismembered Debbie's body. Her grave was a closet, her casket was a plastic container, and her flowers were cement. She was no longer here.

But at that time, nobody except for three people—Louis Colombo, Jason Griffith, and Kalae Casorso, Jason's ex-girlfriend whom he asked to store the container of her body parts—knew she was dead. So her family was on a mission to find her.

A search for Debbie Flores-Narvaez on Facebook still yields results. She died on December 12, 2010, but she was born, as it reads on Facebook, on December 21, 2010, nine days after her death.

The page description reads:

"Debora Flores-Narvaez, a 31-year-old former burlesque dancer for the Luxor's *FANTASY* revue, failed to turn up for a rehearsal on Dec. 13. Speculation over her whereabouts has become a hot topic on the Strip and beyond."

It indeed became a hot topic, and all the news television stations and print media reflected it with their headlines.

And now, the pages reek of sadness and regret. Surely Celeste, the person who posts most often on her sister's page, finds some kind of relief in writing on her wall. As if Debbie, somewhere, somehow, could be reading those posts.

The timeline itself chronicles the entire story. One can gradually see how the posts begin to change in tone up to the point when her body is finally found. Then, everything changes, and the messages are no longer directed to friends and the public at large. They are written exclusively for Debbie.

Every Christmas, Thanksgiving, New Year's Eve, Valentine's Day, and birthday, Debbie gets many messages as a way to keep her alive and current of everything that is happening in her world. When her birthday came around in 2014, as they awaited news of the sentencing, her page was full of comments just as it happens with someone who is alive and has many friends, telling her she would always be in their hearts.

Celeste posted a collage of beautiful pictures with a message that read:

"Happy birthday to the prettiest, most beautiful, compassionate, fun loving Lil Sister in my whole wide world, Debbie Flores-Narvaez. I love you soooo much!!!"

Debbie was a dancer, a model, a performer, and a career woman, and she always loved to write. She loved quotes that had a message. She loved sunflowers, and her page is full of pictures of them.

In December 2013, Celeste posted a picture of Debbie's pink Christmas tree. As psychic Gale St. John had said and Celeste had confirmed, pink was Debbie's favorite color.

"The holidays were Debbie's favorite season. When she left I got all her Christmas stuff including her pink tree. Only Debbie would have a pink tree," Celeste wrote. "So I decided to put it in my office for display. This tree screams Debbie and things she loved to a tee. She has ballerinas, purses, shoes, dresses, stars, snowmen, candy, lollipops, Hello Kitty, sparkles, sequins, Victoria's Secret "Pink" dogs, even a pink Cadillac, all ornaments are pink.

I so love it. As I was putting up each one, so many memories and reminders came to me. I so miss her; it still does hurt knowing she's not here. Love her. . . ."

For their part, Debbie's family and friends were making certain that the slain dancer was not forgotten. They began a blog on Word Press, one that had started off as the bringdebbiehome.com website. The new blog linked to the latter, and showed a photo of Debbie, resting on a tree trunk wearing a yellow sundress. And on it are photos of her favorite flowers, sunflowers.

There was a quote from Debbie's MySpace page, giving readers a very good idea about the nature of the young woman:

I ♥ life. The Arts is my passion in life— Dancing, Modeling and of course Music (in which makes dancing the art that it truly is :) However, it's dancing that has given me many opportunities. I am a Ballroom/Latin Dancer as well as a Hip-Hop dancer. I ♥ modeling and acting just as much. I enjoy good friendships, good company, family, music & playing my guitar :) I earned 3 degrees in college: Bachelor of Science degree in international Business, a Master's degree in Finance and went to Law School and earned my Juris Doctorate degree in Criminal Law. I was born and raised in the beautiful islands of Puerto Rico and lived in Baltimore, Maryland and Washington D.C. for 12 years.

*I am well-cultured, quick witted, intelligent, consid-
erate and humorous. I'm blessed with a substantial
amount of common sense & most say 'too smart' for my
own good :) I am confident, tolerant, loving, realistic,
big-hearted and completely uninterested in shallow pre-
tentious people. I am naturally curious and analytical,
which makes me pretty adventurous and willing to try
almost anything once. I am also very driven, ambitious,
determined and dedicated—qualities that permeate
every aspect of my life. I have broad tastes and interests.
My partner in life is someone willing to jump out of a
plane with me (spontaneous), then relax, watch the sun-
set and just cuddle (romantic and a lover). If there is a
way to be outgoing and tranquil at the same time, I'm
it! It's important to live life to the fullest as you don't
know what tomorrow will bring . . . or if it will be here,
but still have a good outlook and presence for the future.
And as ALWAYS: Remember to . . . ROCK ON. . . .
well Puerto ROCK as they know it :)*

Debbie's mother, Elsie Narvaez, posted in English on
the blog before her daughter was found murdered. In her
post, she calls her "Debbie, my lovely daughter," and tells
her how much she loves her and misses her and always
prayed that God would guide her. Of course, Elsie Narvaez did not yet know her daughter had come to a very
bad end, and she tells her that she prays she will be found

safe and sound so that the family can spend Thanksgiving and Christmas together as always.

Most touching of all, the mother says she prays her daughter will dance again with that "beautiful smile of yours," and cites a favorite quote of Debbie's: "Life isn't about how to survive the storm, but how to dance in the rain." Elsie Narvaez then finds the courage, again, to promise her daughter that they will both be dancing in the rain, and see each other soon.

Her father, Carlos Flores, posted, also in English, that he always loved his daughter and was happy for all the times they talked and laughed together. He tells her he always knew she had "a great talent with the music and the dance," and how proud he was that she took it all to the next level. He, too, tells her he just wants her to come home, so he can see her again, share her smile, and share her dreams. And he also prays for her, he says, and prays that she may continue her dreams. She triumphed where others failed, and despite of her own failures, and in addition to her successes, he says to her, "You'll always be my little Debbie with the beautiful smile."

But the blog turns somber at the following announcement:

"Tragically, the outcome of Debbie Flores-Narvaez is heart-wrenching and difficult to comprehend. Thanks to a brave soul who contacted one of the tip hotlines listed, Debbie's remains have been discovered, recovered, and identified. As you can imagine, the family is devastated. Here is the latest horrific news." The aforementioned was a link to all of the news reports about the outcome, or the murder of Debbie Flores-Narvaez.

Then, another announcement: "Due to the overwhelming response of people around the world, the intense web traffic, and the need for improved functionality, the free Word Press site had to be upgraded and the improved site is now LIVE. Even so, this page will remain online forever because of the many beautiful comments and outpouring of love which have been shared."

On the "live" stream are the endless expressions of sorrow and remembrances by those who knew Debbie well, and even strangers who knew of the death of the dancer who only had one dream: to dance.

EIGHTEEN

◇◇◇

Sentencing

As usual, Celeste shared her thoughts on Facebook the day before the sentencing, on July 22, 2014.

"Heading to Las Vegas tomorrow for final sentencing on the monster who took Debbie's life. I can't believe it's been two months since his conviction of murder and now his final Judgment day of sentencing. I finally finished writing my Victim's Statement on how it has impacted me and my life as a whole since this whole nightmare began. So many things I want to say and express and yet somehow I have to put it in writing and express it with words. How do I do that? How can anyone express that type or ordeal and horror they have been faced with in their life? There are not enough words or time, and yet somehow I managed to put in on paper. I'm feeling nervous, anxious and anguished to have to face him again. But this time I get to tell him what he did to me, what he caused me, what he has put me through, what I've lost! I get to express myself and tell him how I feel, but yet I have to hold back and do it with composure. Oh my God this is going to be the hardest thing in my life I will ever face! JESUS, LORD, GOD, ALMIGHTY SAVIOR please help me get through this with my mental and physical sanity intact!"

A lot of friends and supporters offered words of comfort and encouragement, and Celeste replied to one in particular who told her to ditch the notes and speak from her heart: "I would love to do that, but what is going to guide me is my rage and my feet making their way towards him and wanting to take revenge. So with that being said I'll stick to a personal script to keep me in line."

It would be exactly sixty-two long and sleepless nights for two families between the verdict and the sentencing. It had been two months since Debbie's sister and parents got to see, face-to-face, eye-to-eye, the man who'd killed their dear Debbie, the man who'd cut her life short, the man who'd showed no remorse even when photos of her dismembered corpse were displayed at trial.

They, Debora's family, had been impatiently waiting for this day.

They are a law-abiding, decent family, but they were expecting the worst from the justice system.

The harsher the sentencing, the better they would feel afterward, they hoped.

Once in Las Vegas, Celeste ran into a piece written by Ana Ley for the *Las Vegas Sun*. Its headline read: "Two mothers brace for sentencing in killing of Luxor dancer."

The article appeared in the publication on Tuesday, July 22, 2014, and it set the stage for the first encounter between Charlene Davis and Elsie Narvaez, Jason's and Debbie's mothers, respectively, in the Clark County courtroom on the day of the sentencing.

The two mothers were, of course, at opposite ends of the spectrum as far as the guilt and innocence of the defendant, Jason Omar Griffith. Elsie Narvaez, tearful and angry over the slaying of her youngest daughter, maintained that Debbie's ex-boyfriend had premeditatedly slain the young woman, and she was asking for the harshest possible punishment. Charlene Davis, as one would expect, sided with her son, alleging that it was Debora who had provoked him and he was simply defending himself from a physical onslaught from a strong, trained dancer.

For her part, Narvaez planned on addressing Judge Kathleen Delaney during her victim impact statement. She wanted to make certain that her daughter's killer was sent to jail for the rest of his life.

After sitting through days of testimony, and gruesome accounts, vivid with photographs, of her daughter's dismemberment, Elsie Narvaez still had faith in the justice system, she said.

The paper quoted Narvaez: "Karma will do us justice. We just want this case to end so that we can have some peace of mind. This is not right."

Ms. Ley, court reporter for the *Las Vegas Sun*, also spoke to the defense attorneys, who stated they planned to appeal their client's conviction. Abel Yáñez, Jason Griffith's attorney, told the reporter about the video in his possession, which recorded the fight between Debbie and Jason. The judge had prevented the defense from showing it to the jury, Yáñez said.

Charlene Davis was quoted as saying she was hoping her son would be acquitted completely but was afraid there had been too much press coverage; that the media had been biased and the public and the jurors influenced.

Celeste was irate that Jason Griffith's mother was what she called "delusional," and Debbie's sister had not believed there actually would be appeals. But a mother is, after all, a mother, and as a mother, Charlene Davis was now grieving for her son just as Celeste and her mother grieved for Debbie.

Several of Jason Griffith's coworkers and friends had written letters of support to Judge Kathleen Delaney on his behalf. They are reproduced here, also as part of the public records, and Abel Yáñez, Griffith's attorney, also gave me a copy of the letters, now part of the public record, sent to the judge. There are always two sides to every story. This story seems a bit like *Rashomon*, the Japanese movie about a rape and a murder told from three different vantage points: the wife, the husband, and the robber.

One of the letters was written by Susannah Denney, a child artist coordinator for the Beatles' *LOVE* show at the time when Jason used to perform. She says they met in 2008, when he joined the cast.

"Mr. Griffith and I worked together during rehearsals, performances and Cirque sponsored events. He always carried himself as a true professional, timely and prepared for all that was required of him. It was a pleasure to work with Mr. Griffith. He was an outstanding role model for the young performers in my charge," Susannah wrote.

The child performers play an important role in the development of the storyline for this spectacular and exclusive Las Vegas show. Susannah Denney worked with Jason and around the children, and she appeared to be very pleased with the way he interacted with the minors in that professional environment. I can only imagine how difficult it must be, because, after all, it is work and people pay hundreds of dollars to watch such a prestigious performance. Every act, every performance, must be flawless.

"Oftentimes you could find him cracking jokes and making the boys feel valued as contributing members of the cast," she said.

All of the letters Judge Kathleen Delaney received were presented by the defense on behalf of Jason's friends and colleagues. All of them agreed in one way or another that Jason Griffith was a "very dependable, focused and responsible employee."

Those were the exact words written by Tina Cannon, Jason's partner at *LOVE*. They had met two and a half years before Griffith's arrest, through their employment at the show. She referred to him as a "friend as well as a coworker." Just like in any other discipline, a working partner should always be someone you trust. Tina said she trusted Jason Griffith.

"I felt safe, and I could always trust him. He treated me with respect, gentleness, took corrections well. It was easy to talk to him and communicate any necessary adjustments that needed to be made," she stated.

Tina Cannon also had a personal friendship with the dancer. She describes him as a good communicator, a listener, and a peacemaker, saying, "Jason was a good and caring friend.

"He often would listen to both sides of the story, help us [Tina and her boyfriend] understand the other person, and then offer advice. He was patient and always available if I called him on the phone upset or needed to ask his advice on things."

Another letter came from one of Griffith's very close friends, Laura Jane Kirkham.

In her letter, she begs the magistrate to show leniency on Jason Griffith's behalf for numerous reasons. "Mainly because I miss my friend. He has been changed by prison prior to this trial and has become increasingly remorseful and deeply distraught by his time served already. He is such a laid back individual and prior to this horribly tragic situation had nothing but love for everyone," she said. Even after everything he admitted to having done, his friend sees him as a victim, not as a murderer.

"It is a terrible situation that the laws which were supposed to protect innocent individuals, I believe let them down. I sat present every day during trial and was astonished that Jason was put through so much in his personal life, I was only made aware of the situation back in September 2010 when I approached Jason to help me choreograph a dance and the music for my wedding as well as participate and join me in my special day.

"Jason's words that day will forever haunt me. Jason looked at me in the eye when I started to beg for him to come with me and stated 'I can't help you or come because Debbie will follow me there and I would feel awful for ruining your special day.'"

In contrast to those hoping for leniency, both Celeste and her mother, Elsie Narvaez, stated they would be highly upset if Judge Kathleen Delaney gave Griffith the minimum sentence of ten years instead of the maximum sentence of twenty-five years without parole. Still, the sister who had been through it all—the search for Debbie, the trial's postponements, the trial itself, and now another wait for the sentence—now had to listen to the final words from both sides, and once more, relive her little sister's murder.

Just as it had been on the day Jason Griffith was found guilty of second-degree murder, court started at 9 A.M. sharp on July 23, 2014, in the Las Vegas Regional Justice Center, the same room that witnessed an intense almost two weeks of arguments, lies, pain, tears, and thirst for revenge during the murder trial.

During the trial Jason Griffith had looked like a young executive or a grad student. Now he was walking with his hands behind his body as he entered the courtroom dressed in a black V-neck old jumpsuit that revealed his neck tattoo.

His hands were shackled.

He faced several charges: murder, domestic violence, and destruction of evidence in the death of Debora Flores-Narvaez.

Celeste's anxiety was palpable even through the words she posted to Facebook. "Here we go. . . . Glad to see that he's already dressed in his prison uniform! God be with me and my family," she wrote.

Jason Griffith, for his part, appealed before the judge on his own behalf. He pleaded with Judge Kathleen Delaney: "In tomorrow's paper, the novelists who claim to be journalists won't report the things that you really know. I asked twelve jurors to help me and give me back my freedom but they didn't know the things that you know. I asked the police fourteen times to help me and they didn't know the things that you know. So today, Judge, I'm asking for a fifteenth time, will you help me?" he begged, trying to look at the magistrate eye-to-eye, hoping at least for a modicum of compassion.

Griffith's defense attorney, Abel Yáñez, again tried to convince the judge that his client had killed Debbie in self-defense.

"In their relationship, it was Flores-Narvaez who was violent. I've yet to hear any evidence that Jason has been violent to Debbie or that Jason has been violent in any of his prior relationships. She was a deeply troubled person who probably needed mental health treatment. She did not deserve to die, but Jason had the right to defend himself," Yáñez still argued.

Judge Delaney reminded Griffith's team that the trial was over and the self-defense argument was no longer relevant. But she had expressed this at the very beginning, that the murder did not fit the category of self-defense.

Jason Griffith went on: "I'm saddened by these events and everyone these events have affected." That was the closest he came to offering an apology to the family for strangling and dismembering Debbie.

"You knew she had convictions for stalking and second

degree assault. We all know that if I were a woman and I were accosted by a man like this, I would not be standing here today," Griffith said to the judge.

Griffith's comments did not sit well with Judge Delaney, who placed the blame solely on the defendant. The judge did not hold back her opinion of who she thought Jason was as a person, as a man. "The responsibility for this toxic and ultimately tragic relationship continuing as long as it did is entirely yours," said Judge Delaney. "You knew who Debbie was and you knew who she hoped you would be. But you also knew you were never going to be that person. The only reason I can see is to satisfy your own narcissistic predisposition."

Griffith looked down, much like a child who has been punished without recess. He realized he was losing the battle for his life.

Celeste Flores-Narvaez trained her eyes on Jason like lasers.

After the sentence was read, then came what everyone was waiting for, her victim's statement.

She prefaced it by saying: "This statement was written all towards Jason 'Blu' Griffith. For me to look him face to face and tell him everything I wanted him to know. For me to face him after all these tears and tell him how I felt about what he did to me and my family. But I found out that the Nevada Clark County Court would not allow me to directly talk to him or look at him. I had to direct my Victim's Statement towards the court and the judge. I was not happy about that at all. So I had to change all the 'yous' to 'he', 'him', also 'evil' and 'murderer.'" She later said, "I had to keep it professional. I couldn't say what I really wanted to!"

Here is her statement, as she read it to a silent and stunned courtroom. She sent it to Diana via e-mail:

I have been waiting for this day since December 15th 2010. I remember speaking to you like it was just yesterday. I remember the nonchalant sound of your voice. I remember your cold demeanor. I remember the conversation. I knew from the first conversation we had that it was you! Every single day for the past three and a half years and I'm sure for the rest of my life I think and will think about that moment.

I often wonder on a daily basis whether I made the right choice. You see, I believe in an eye for an eye punishment. But I also believe that sometimes the justice system works to put criminals away and for victims and families to receive the justice deserved and some type of closure. Also giving them inner peace that someone doesn't fall victim under evil's hands again. I won't lie. It's hard for me to stand here now and still not want to take justice into my own hands and personally do to you what you did to my little sister Debbie. It's taking every fiber and depth of my soul to hold my composure. Especially since I always stood up for her and was there for her when she had a problem growing up. The guilt that I feel is unbearable. And regardless of what I did for her to help find her and help bring her justice, it will never be enough in my eyes.

But I have a choice! Between good and evil! Right or wrong! Heaven or Hell. And I choose not to be like you and not take matters into my own hands.

I choose to follow the laws and for the justice system to work its course and I'm praying that I choose the right path and for the system to work in our favor. And I'm praying that you will suffer behind bars for the maximum sentence the law can possibly give you. I made Debbie that promise. Her birthday was just two weeks ago and what a great birthday present it would be for her if I followed through on that promise.

Three years ago to date, I went to work as I normally do, performing as I normally do. Thought about the Christmas season and all the many gifts I had to purchase for my family. The thought of the errands and pressure from the holiday season began to consume me. Nothing out of the ordinary, just another manic Friday. After completing my daily schedule, I proceed to pick up my children in rush hour traffic. I had to make a stop at the local grocery store. At the time my children, Izeyah was 12 and Mycah was just a year old. I pulled up to my house, grabbed the groceries and my children and plunged head first into my motherly duties.

As I proceeded to the door my cell phone rang, I saw who the caller was and answered. At that time Izeyah was misbehaving in school. After many different methods of punishment he still managed to be disobedient. I'd finally given him the ultimate punishment, no Christmas! It's a child's worst punishment, I thought. I was fed up and had to set an example to my son showing him how I would not tolerate his misbehavior and lack of scholastic excellence. I was comfortable and stern in my decision. I was going to stick to it. My mother disapproved and thought I was being too harsh. We had gotten into an argument about it days prior and I wasn't speaking to her for a couple of days. So when I got that phone call I knew for certain it was in reference to my son. The caller was Debbie. She was calling about wanting to send presents for Izeyah and Mycah. Of course I knew right away she was going to try to disregard my punishment for my son agreeing with my mother attempting to talk me out of it. I was tired from work and I was consumed with grocery bags yet I spoke briefly with her. Just as I thought, she was trying to change my mind. I concluded the conversation by telling her, "I will call you back so we can talk about it later."

That was the last time I spoke with her. The last time

I heard her voice. The last chance I had to tell her "I Love You." You see, I never called her back. Not because I forgot or didn't have time to. I simply didn't want to. I didn't want to talk to her about my son's punishment, presents and certainly not the stresses of Christmas. Looking back today it was something so silly that was worth calling her back and talking about, but I never did. . . . That's a decision I punish myself for to date.

I was forced to learn never take time or life for granted. Never assume you'll always have a next time. Act on the moment, because once those moments are gone they are gone forever. I learned those words the hard way.

My next call about Debbie was the following week from both of my parents. The day my life would change forever, the day my nightmare would begin. The day the devil's work would break my heart and take part of my world with him. The day my family and I became victims. The day our happiness and innocence was annihilated by the dishonor of evil hands.

Evil made sure you took Debbie's last breath. He decided to play God and take the power of her life into his own hands for his own selfish reasons. He decided when it was her time to go and end it. He wrapped his hands around her neck, and watch second by second throughout the minutes as she took her last breath until she was gone and her body lay lifeless. He proceeded with gruesome acts to her small-framed body disposing of her as if she was nothing. He intended for no one to ever find or see her again. He lied and deceived everyone, beginning with Debbie and ending with me and everyone in between.

All while watching me suffer, pleading for help, hearing my cries, seeing my pain and desperation on her whereabouts. "Where's was my little sister," I would ask. "Please help me find her," I would beg. No one else knew, but he and his roommate certainly did. However, he was preoccupied with disposing of her remains.

Evil made sure he took me and my family, friends, detectives and the city of Las Vegas desperate, stressed without answers for days and weeks. But he failed, he's a failure! His intentions to murder her and make her disappear without a trace weren't comparable to the love I have for her. The bond between my sister and I would never stop me from finding her and the truth. I would've stopped at nothing in doing all that I possibly could to help find her. She was my one and only little sister. And he took that from me. From the moment I spoke with him and heard his voice on the same day my nightmare began, I knew it was him! Without a doubt it was him! Not for a moment did he fool me like he did to others.

I would have gone to hell and back to make sure I found her. To witness his judgment day, paying for what he did to her! You see, he became my nightmare and I still live in it. However, I made sure I became his nightmare where he would reside in hell.

His actions came as an unwanted liability to me. He robbed my family and me of the opportunity to bid her farewell. The many holidays, lifetime memories, sibling agreements, disagreements and everything in between are no longer afforded. He took a premature relationship between my children and their aunt away at their innocence. My only sister, who I quietly envied and admired for all her accomplishments and accolades. I never got the chance to tell her how jealous and proud I was of her for going after her dreams. He took her from her lifelong friends. He cancelled all her dreams and future plans. He took my last I love you, a soft kiss on her forehead and a warm reassuring sisterly hug.

He took it all. . . .

But don't get me wrong, not only was he selfish. He was also a big giver. You see, he gave me and my family nightmares and countless sleepless nights. It's now three and a half years later, and our sleepless nights are still tallying. He has showered me with stress, sorrow, hurt, anger, anxiety, grief, shock, nervousness, suffering, fright, hatred, and great mental and physical anguish. In fact, every possible type of pain and emotion a human soul could possibly bear and handle. He also attempted to stare me down while in court with a look in his face of disbelief, as if how dare I look at you with such disgust. My answer is simple: because you are worthless. He is worthless to me and my family and society as we know it. He is a non-factor. As of today, he will no longer exist to society. He will be just a number in the system of criminals.

Debbie loved her family, she loved her friends; she loved her nephews. She always did everything she could for others. She loved to dance and entertain. And she was always successful in pursuing her dreams with great accomplishments until he took it all away; he took it away from her, her family, my sons and from me. But he robbed her of all that. She doesn't get to smile, or laugh, or cry or see or feel the things she loved the most anymore. She also doesn't get to do and enjoy what she loved the most. But he does. Even behind bars he is still able to wake up every day and see the light of the sun and other faces. He gets to talk to his family and have them visit him. He gets to have small talk and conversation. He gets to cry and smile and even laugh at jokes from time to time. He even gets to hear an occasional "I love you" from a loved one. He still has all those abilities because he has life even though he's not deserving of it. It hurts me that he gets to enjoy small things in life. Sometimes those actually matter the most.

I will really hope and pray that he receives the maximum sentencing without parole. For every single day he spends in his 6x8 cell that he gets to really enjoy dancing, entertaining and performing for his fellow inmates while he's locked up behind those walls.

◇◇◇

There was not a dry eye in the courtroom as Celeste Flores-Narvaez, the older sister of the slain dancer, walked back to her seat, with her head held high and looking back at her killer with the utmost disdain.

As she later said, with some degree of satisfaction: "Yeah, I apparently had everyone in the courtroom in tears, even the cameramen. I wasn't aware of it until after court and I was being interviewed. But I did notice the judge becoming red in the face as she was about to tear up, but she held back. It was very hard for me to say what I felt throughout all those years and put it on paper. I wasn't sure if I was going to be able to or not until days before. The crazy thing was the intro (first three paragraphs) I wrote in my closet the night before I left to court while looking for my shoes. I sat and wrote it into my phone. And then had to copy and paste it and send it to the court's e-mail to have it print up and add it twenty minutes before court started. I had so much I wanted to say. But not enough words to express what I went through."

As expected, the courtroom was full of reporters and photographers who all wanted to get the best reaction shot possible, the best view of the victim's family as the sentencing was read as well as the murderer's face as he received his punishment. The television news all knew this would be the opening story for their newscasts that night, so they scrambled to get a good sound bite, a good shot that captured the moment better than anybody else's.

Sitting down on the side of the prosecution were Debbie's immediate family, and all those who, without even knowing Debbie in person, had become close to the case and felt as if their presence was needed for moral support for the Flores-Narvaez family.

The family was dressed as if they were attending a funeral. Carlos Flores, Debbie's father, wore a black suit. Celeste, her mother, Elsie, and two friends of the family were also all wearing black.

On the other side of the courtroom, the benches were almost empty; only a couple of people, and Charlene Davis, Jason Griffith's mother. She was always there for her son, which was easy to understand. To a mother, a son never stops being the most important person in her life. He never stops being her baby.

But just as we might never truly know what was in her son's head on the day he murdered his ex-girlfriend, no one except the man himself would ever grasp what he'd been thinking during these past couple of weeks, awaiting his sentencing. At some point, he'd even been placed under a suicide watch again.

On this day, he was standing before a woman, a judge upholding the highest law of the land; a woman who now had in her hands the future he had worked for so arduously.

The victim's family addressed Griffith, pressing the judge for the maximum sentence.

Debbie's father, Carlos Flores, said: "The only thing we have left is memories, photographs, and video clips. We won't have our daughter back."

Trying to maintain her composure, Elsie Narvaez addressed the judge, asking her for the maximum sentence. She did so in English, with a heavy Puerto Rican accent and tears in her eyes.

"Jason Omar Griffith needs to stay in prison for a long time, long time. We love and miss our daughter. She's our rainbow in the sky." Elsie even told the judge that Debbie was a registered organ donor, something she couldn't even do after her death, because of the condition in which her body was left.

"That was the day that the devil's work would break my heart and take apart my world," said Celeste in tears.

It was difficult for all of those present in the courthouse, hearing the voice of a desperate woman and a broken family.

"No more phone calls, or birthday cards telling me happy birthday, Mom," Elsie said.

Dressed in her judge's garb, and in a very assertive tone after hearing both sides, the judge read her sentence:

"It is my determination to adjudicate you guilty at this time with a murder of second degree and sentence you to the maximum sentence of life in prison."

The Flores family held hands, cried, and were visibly touched as they finally found some closure after so much pain. A wave of relief swept through the family as they heard the sentencing.

Jason Griffith turned to his mother, who had stood by her son throughout the case. Charlene Davis told her son, tearfully, "I will fight this every day until I get back to you. I adore you."

The sentencing immediately made headlines across the state and the country, from Fox News to the *Las Vegas Sun*, from the Minneapolis *Star Tribune* to the *Huffington Post*.

Celeste created her own headlines in her Facebook page a few hours later:

I'm happy with the outcome of a life sentence because I know he will not get the chance at parole. Debbie can now rest in peace with justice served. This maximum was 25 but the judge gave him life, with eligibility for parole after that. I want to take the time to THANK EVERYONE OF YOU. Everyone from the LVPD, detectives, DA Office, courts, judge. The media who worked hard and kept her alive. But I especially want to thank, the volunteers, city and community of Las Vegas who embraced me and my family. Her friends, my friends and supporters who have stood by my side since day one. You gave me strength when I was weak. Positive reinforcement when I was down and helped me back up. And so many prayers that they made a huge difference in today's outcome. The power of prayers and God does exist. Thank you all so much. There are not enough words that I can give you for my gratitude. Love you guys. Xoxoxo.

Later that same day after Jason Griffith was sentenced, longtime Las Vegas news reporter Aaron Drawhorn from the local CBS station was able to get a short and peculiar interview with him from behind bars.

Aaron is a tall, blond, green-eyed, handsome young man from Port Neches, Texas, whom I first met when we both worked as journalists in Texas. Later, when I moved to Las Vegas for my Univision job, the first reporter I bumped into out in the field was Aaron.

Las Vegas is a crazy, fast-paced, and bustling city for tourists, but for locals, it is a small town. Locals hang out in the same spots, almost always trying to escape from the tourists and the madness at the Strip. Every time a new restaurant or bar opens, it gets packed with the same people. Again, with the locals; the tourists don't know about such spots.

Aaron was friends with Chris, an Australian guy who lived at the Onyx Apartments, the same apartment complex as Debbie and her roommate, Sonya. He recalled that

Chris had always been mentioning his neighbor who talked finance but also danced in the *FANTASY* show at the Luxor.

The reporter clearly remembered the day the story broke, about "a missing girl from *FANTASY* who had many college degrees," he said. "It didn't take very long for me to piece everything together," he said, since "what were the odds of a *FANTASY* dancer, who had a master's degree in finance and who also lived at the Onyx Apartments?" he asked himself. It was certainly an odd combination, and a little more than a coincidence, he thought. By this time, his friend Chris, the one who lived in the same apartment building as Debbie and Sonya, had moved back to Australia. Aaron sent him a private message via Facebook.

A couple of days went by, and Aaron finally got a reply from Chris, apologizing for not responding sooner. Chris told him he was aware of the case because their building manager had already contacted him to tell him that Debora was missing. The two friends, although now far away, exchanged a couple of messages. Aaron kept the Australian posted on all the developments on the case.

"It was one of the most high profile murders that Las Vegas had seen in years," Aaron remarked. "It isn't every day that an entertainer on the Strip goes missing." Many more reporters than usual covered it; sometimes there was not even a seat in the courtroom, he recalled. "Debbie's murder got as much attention as the O.J. Simpson robbery and kidnapping trial in Vegas," he observed.

"One thing about this trial and Griffith that was different was that Jason talked on the stand." Aaron assumed the defendant thought that if he was going to get a break or any sort of sympathy from this gruesome murder it was going to be with his testimony.

"At the end, it kind of did," was Aaron's theory about the outcome. "The jury came to second-degree rather than first-degree murder. It had to be his testimony that got him a lesser conviction."

Still, Aaron remembered that Jason Griffith had been argumentative on the stand.

"At one point the prosecutor asked him a question and his reply was: 'Seriously?' That stuck with me," he observed. Aaron also remembered that a lot of courtroom watchers agreed that if Griffith had called the police right away, he would've had a much stronger self-defense case. But he hadn't done that. And to top it off, Griffith blamed it on the methods of the Las Vegas Police Department when he said Metro was "shoot first, ask questions later." Not to mention that he'd face charges of concealment and disposing of the body.

Aaron was not surprised that Jason Griffith got a hard sentence from the bench.

The same afternoon, after the sentencing was handed down, Aaron and his photographer were made aware that

Griffith was available for a media interview. His assignment desk chief called him. Everyone—meaning every news media outlet—was there, his superior told him.

"I get down there, and we were first in line. Channel 3 is next, but I had a first shot at him."

An officer at the Clark County Detention Center told him to set up in a booth where Jason Griffith would meet and talk with him via telephone through a glass.

"Our camera was set up right in front of his space. We were rolling as soon as I sat down and I said hello."

But Griffith had wanted to do the interview face-to-face, "on his terms." When the camera started rolling behind a wall made of glass in the Clark County Detention Center, Griffith did not seem very happy.

"This whole yellow journalism, this whole 'you look guilty in this setting, you look like an animal, like a monster that people cannot come and touch you.' That's not who I am, and that is how I have been depicted since the beginning of this, so I am really not interested in doing it this way," Jason Griffith said.

He was concerned about his "image" during the interview.

"It is a bit early for me with the things I want to share with you guys. I wanted a little bit of time to digest what just happened today," he told the reporter.

Aaron said he spent the next few minutes basically arguing with the prisoner about the interview, and although Jason Griffith was very polite, he was extremely upset about the forum of the interview.

According to Aaron, Griffith apparently did not want to do it through a glass and on the telephone, but "he had no choice. You have to get approval from the jail administration to do a face-to-face interview. The media outlet must request approval and it takes going up a chain of command to interview an inmate face-to-face."

Griffith told Aaron he wanted what is known as a "contact visit," or in person and face-to-face, because he felt that when the public saw him speaking through a telephone behind a glass, it would make him look like a criminal. He indicated to Aaron, he did not like the way he was being portrayed in the media.

"This went on back and forth between us for about seven minutes," the reporter said. "At one point, Griffith acknowledged that we were having an interview about an interview." However, Jason Griffith never asked their crew to stop recording.

After coming to a grinding halt and a dead end, Aaron asked Griffith to please answer a couple of questions, taking the opportunity that the media was already there waiting, but he declined.

Aaron asked if Griffith thought he'd had a fair trial, or felt he'd been wrongly portrayed in the media, but Griffith still would not elaborate.

"He said he needed more time to think about a couple

of things he wanted to talk about," Aaron remembered, at which point the reporter, feeling a tad exasperated, retorted, "You had enough time."

By this point, Aaron realized the interview was not going to happen. He knew he had enough to get two sound bites for this story, and he basically concluded the conversation.

No one else who was waiting was able to obtain an interview at all.

Aaron said he'd even told Griffith that there was another television station in line to speak with him, as a courtesy to his colleague, but apparently the prisoner hadn't wanted to go another round and argue with another reporter.

Nor has he spoken to anyone since, presumably, as of this writing.

As of that day, July 23, 2014, Jason "Blu" Omar Griffith will pay, with every day that remains of his natural life, for what he did to Debora Flores-Narvaez on the night of December 12, 2010. He is eligible for possible parole after ten years, counting the three he already served. This means that in 2021, he can appear before a parole board and request to be set free on parole.

But then, there is that pesky matter of the family appearing at his parole hearings, especially Celeste, the sister who had so adamantly pleaded for a harsh sentence. Celeste, as usual, posted her reaction to the sentence on Facebook, after a hiatus, to let family and friends that she was holding up okay.

"So ever since that bastard was sentenced to life in prison for Debbie. I feel like a different person. I know I will have to deal with this again in regards to an appeal, parole, etc. But I feel like a ton has been lifted off my chest. I feel more at peace & relaxed. I smile a lil more & less stressed, even happier. They say God will not give you what you cannot handle. And that's sooo true. I'm a testament to that. Amen!

"But please let God decide what I can & cannot handle. I love my family & friends. I do. They're all I got when I leave to pass on my existence.

"And I know that they love me and mean well and try to protect me from things. . . ."

NINETEEN

✦✦✦

Dreams and Messages

Let me preface what I'm going to tell you by first saying that I'm a very skeptical, yet open-minded woman.

Growing up in Colombia until the age of thirteen, I always heard stories about people who could somehow communicate with loved ones who have passed away. This belief is prevalent in our Latin countries. But it had never happened to me until this day, and I am not even sure if it did all.

As a journalist, I'm used to hearing the most harrowing stories and looking at disturbing graphic images, but I've always tried to leave them "at work," before I got home to my husband and my pets.

Nevertheless, Debbie's story has been different. There are times when I have been working day and night talking about her, to her friends, family, or the authorities, so it has been almost impossible not to take the work home, since every time I write, it has to be at my house because I do not have the time to do it at work.

That being said, I'm not sure if it is that my brain is overworked and in overdrive, or if Debbie really has tried to connect with me. Talking to her sister, she has mentioned similar things happening to her; she says she feels Debbie's presence.

The first couple of days after she was found dead, I would often feel as if someone was in the car with me.

Now, almost four years later, and now that I am also getting more details about Jason Griffith's life, I felt it again.

It was a couple of days ago as of this writing that it happened, the day I interviewed Griffith's attorney Abel Yáñez. I got home hoping to write as much as I could for the book. It is always better to write down information when it is "fresh," especially because you don't leave as many small details behind.

But there came a point when I felt like I had to stop writing. It was about to stop around 1 A.M., and it felt as if Debbie were there; it felt uncomfortable as I kept on reproducing the information I'd been given by Yáñez—that Debora was a stalker, the appeal and the possible grounds for it, and the fact that Griffith said her murder was self-defense. The next night, I was able to finally play the video that Jason Griffith had recorded, of Debbie admitting to the acts of petty vandalism.

Judge Kathleen Delaney had suppressed the videos from being shown at Jason Griffith's murder trial, although in them, Debbie does admit that she assaulted Griffith, broke into his house, looked on his laptop, poured egg whites on his car, and slashed three of his car tires. She says she knows what is wrong under the law.

Abel Yáñez, Jason's attorney, had talked about this video for a while. The defense tried to enter the black-and-white recording as evidence during the *Nevada vs. Jason Omar Griffith* trial, but Judge Delaney refused once and again for it to be part of the evidence. She objected because the video had been recorded secretly in Griffith's bedroom sometime in 2010, a couple of months before Griffith ended Debora's life. The original video was longer, but Griffith had edited the recording down to 1 minute and 34 seconds. Delaney denied the attorney's petition for it to be played to the jury, saying any statement should always be listened to or read in its entirely, so the jury could have a clear understanding of the exact scenario, not only the parts Jason Griffith wanted to be heard.

Yáñez, however, believed the video was a key element to show how Debbie supposedly assaulted his client, so during my recent visit to Las Vegas where I met with the attorney for coffee, he provided me a copy after the trial was over and the sentence was read. It was saved in a weird format; one had to have a code to download it, which nobody in the newsroom could decipher. So I had to place it in different computers until it finally played. It was chilling to hear Debbie's voice, to hear the desperation in her words, to analyze her body language as she walked back and forth, touched her face, placed her hands on her hips, trying to convince Jason she was right, and that she was, as prosecutor Michelle Fleck had stated, seeking the truth.

During the recording, Griffith seemed very calm. Of course, he, unlike Debbie, knew that they were being recorded. He kept on asking the same question in different ways to Debbie during a heated argument: "So, you admit to having assaulted me?" She was brutally honest and said yes to all his questions, admitting to slashing his car tires, looking on his computer, and pouring egg whites on his car.

To be honest, it was chilling to watch this video for the first time, to see Debbie so full of life, to hear her voice for the first time. I had done so much research and talked about her to so many people that just hearing her was shocking to me. I tell everyone, even her sister, that I feel like I really knew Debbie.

This is a transcript of the 1 minute and 34 second video that defense attorney Abel Yáñez gave me:

Debbie: I'm admitting that I hit you, that I looked in your house, that I looked in your laptop, that I poured egg whites on your car, that I slashed three of your tires because I said, I will give him one left. . . . I am not going to lie about anything that I am doing.

(She starts raising her voice, sounding desperate. If the defense wanted to portray Debbie as an aggressor, the videos would have been proof to the contrary. Debbie does not seem evil, not even mean-spirited, in the videos. She only sounds sincere.)

Debbie: But I did it because you—
Jason: (interrupts) You are doing this because I can't prove it.
Debbie: No. Do you think I'm slashing tires and think you wouldn't know . . . you knew it was me when you walked out. . . .
Jason: But you made sure that there is no proof that you did it, so I can't take any legal action.
Debbie: Blu, fuck with me legally all you want and you will lose? No, I don't fuck with that mentality.

Debbie: I know legally, the law, and I know what it is legally wrong, and what it is legally right.

Jason: Slashing tires is not legally wrong?

Debbie: It is damage to property that no one witnessed.

Jason: So, you are admitting to property damage?

Debbie: Yeah . . . I am admitting it.

This recording is now part of the State of Nevada's public record trial. After Jason was arrested in January 2011, the Las Vegas Police Department seized his home located in North Las Vegas and confiscated his personal computer. This video was found, as well as many other pieces of evidence, so the public defender's office considered it to be useful for their defense. Once again, this was never played to the jury. They only heard of its existence.

As a woman, I've put myself many times in Debbie's shoes. This video, to me, only shows a desperate woman in love, trying to do whatever it took to get her lover's attention. By slashing tires, she screamed, in the wrong ways, I love you. She was begging for her lover's respect and commitment.

The camera is hidden, so the viewer can only see Jason Griffith's back wearing a hoodie. He is sitting down on the right-hand side of a bed with white sheets, and Debbie is standing, wearing sweatpants and a jacket, with her black hair loose, on the left side of the bed.

I asked Yáñez if it wasn't against the law to record someone without their knowledge or consent, and he said it was perfectly fine because his client had done it at the privacy of his house. But then, what was Jason Griffith's purpose in recording evidence? Covering his own back when he got rid of her?

I had to replay the videos many times to understand what was being said and to be able to write a transcript of it. That same night, I had a really vivid dream about Debora.

We are in my car and I believe it is in Las Vegas. I am driving and Debbie is in the front passenger's seat. We talk and I remember seeing her so clear, her hair, her eyes, it didn't seem like a dream. I remember telling her, "Debbie, I feel like I know you. If this hadn't happened to you, I have a feeling we would have had a good friendship."

When I woke up, I was scared, it was about 4 A.M., and my room was dark. I managed to go back to sleep, but when I awoke again, I could not remember much more of what we said. I know she told me "I had two purposes in life. One ended, and I am working on the second." What could that possibly mean? I asked myself.

The next night, I had the opportunity to connect with psychic Gale St. John. It was late, since I am on the West Coast and Gale lives in Toledo, Ohio, but I was told she would be awake so I made the phone call right away.

Gale is a renowned psychic who traipses throughout

the country searching for the missing and presumed dead. She does not charge for her services, and she does it accompanied by her certified cadaver search dogs, which are border collies, the best search dogs there are. She loves them, and they are also pet dogs who live in her home.

Gale St. John had spoken with Celeste Flores-Narvaez on an Internet radio show about Debbie. She has been on such national programs as *Nancy Grace*, *Issues with Jane Velez-Mitchell*, and *Larry King Live*. Gale is a special woman. More than 70 percent of the bodies she has helped to be discovered were people murdered by someone they loved.

But Gale is not one of those psychics who try to grab the media spotlight, nor does she say about someone missing, as other psychics usually do, that the victim will be found "in the woods by a body of water." In fact, she does not like to know anything about a victim beforehand, and does not like the media to interfere with her searches.

I told Gale: "I don't believe in any of this stuff, and I could be just obsessed with so much work, but I am very curious to know if you feel Debbie has tried to send me a message. Does she think I should talk to someone else about her story? Is there anything I'm missing that she wants told?"

I had never spoken to Gale over the phone. She has a very soothing yet confident voice. I felt as though I knew her, and she was happy to take my call even at that late hour. It was 9:30 P.M. my time, and 12:30, after midnight, where she lives. But she knew about Debora's case from previously speaking with Celeste, so she was familiar with all of the details.

We spoke for over forty minutes. I was driving home from work when we started talking. I couldn't even get out of the car; I continued our chat inside my vehicle parked in front of my house. I was so intrigued. At times, I would feel goose bumps while the psychic gave me Debora's message.

"No one knows what happened to Debora," Gale said for openers. "No one knows how much she suffered. The most important thing she wants is to send a message to other women: this could have been you."

She went on to emphasize, to me, I don't know why: "This could have been you, Carolina." These were reminiscent of the words that Marci Gee, one of Jason Griffith's ex-girlfriends, had said to me.

My heart stopped, and I thought, *Is Debbie trying to tell me this?* But I continued listening to Gale.

She said Debbie wanted people to know she wasn't a crazy person and that she was a pretty normal woman for her age.

Apparently, Debbie was very happy to know I was writing a book that does justice to her story.

"This isn't any more about how she was killed. It is

about using the facts of what happened as a lesson, saying, 'Look, is this going on in your life?'"

Gale went on to tell me that Debora feels very close to me, and that she's very thankful she's being portrayed in the right light in this book.

"Her obsession [Jason Griffith] turned out to be her worst nightmare," Gale said. "She chose to overlook it and hide it."

She certainly did hide it; even her sister, Celeste, has told me she never heard about Jason Griffith, or the fact that he was abusive to her.

"Debbie takes responsibility for her actions; she knows where she went wrong," the psychic went on.

I told Gale I feel my cat, Pippa, acts weird at night, something she never did before. It seems to me like she's playing with someone in the living room. I wake up and my kitty is playing with her toys. This happens almost every night I go to bed late working on Debbie's case.

Gale told me cats have a very high sensibility to spirits; more than dogs, she said.

"Has Debbie forgiven Jason?" I asked her.

"No, but she knows she has to," Gale said calmly. "Forgiveness is part of the other side. She understands him."

Gale St. John also said that this time, Debbie "was very calm, unlike the way I heard her before, so playful and animated. Today it felt like jumping hurdles. The way in which she was putting things to me, they weren't real. When things are happening so fast and suddenly there is a resolution, it's like wham! It's the feeling she has. The sentencing was the final outcome of what happened."

The psychic explained, "She was fighting, and trying to make things go in this direction, because she was a hell of a fighter in life. Now she realizes she can't come back, and she has passed, she has crossed over. I heard her kind of whisper: 'Even life cannot bring back life.'

"Tonight I didn't see pink pearls like I did before. Tonight I saw white pearls as she laid them across her own tombstone. It was sad; it was like she was saying, 'Now I'm done, now I have no purpose.' I was driving home from a training session with the dogs while she was speaking to me, and I was actually crying, I was so sad. But I said to her, 'Listen, Debbie, you do have purpose. You had purpose in life and you now have purpose in the spirit world. You can help others cross who have come from the same circumstances you did, and help them. And I know this is not the last time you and I will speak.'"

Debbie's older sister, Celeste, has shown that she and Debbie still manage to "speak" in a way as well:

"OMG my little sister, Debbie, paid me a visit at work," she wrote recently on Facebook. "They say that when you find a feather out of nowhere, out of place where there shouldn't be any. It means an angel or a loved one is with you.

"I work in an office. No birds at all obviously. It wasn't there yesterday. I look down underneath my desk by my feet and there's a feather. My mom finds them from time to time *in* her house.

"Thanks, Debbie. I needed to know you were with me today. I miss you. . . ."

EPILOGUE

"Everything happens for a reason." We've all heard this saying so many times throughout our lives, right? In some cases, we just roll our eyes. But in most of them, as time goes on, one realizes that this is a very appropriate saying. In this case, it was destiny.

I remember working on this case day and night. As the events unfolded, it was one of those cases where everything was a mystery; it was not predictable at all. I also never expected to get a message from my colleague Diego Arias asking me if I wanted to write a book with longtime and well-known writer Diana Montané.

I clearly remember that day. I was driving with my husband while talking with Diana over the phone for over two hours. At the end of the conversation, we felt like we had known each other for years. I told her everything I knew about the investigation, and it just became our obsession.

We both felt we needed to tell Debbie's story: her life, her dreams, and the tragic events that ended her life so abruptly.

Diana tells me I am her Colombian daughter, and I tell her not only she is my second mom, but my angel.

Over the course of three years, I've experienced long and sleepless nights not only writing, researching, but also thinking about Debbie.

People ask me all the time how difficult it is to cover so many horrible stories, how I sleep at night after hearing all the terrible testimonies of victims of a crime. The truth is I cannot picture myself doing anything else. At the end of the day, if I can make a difference in someone's life with my work, I think I've accomplished my mission.

Everything happens for a reason, right? Ever since we started this book, we thought, this should be a movie, and Roselyn Sanchez would be perfect to play Debbie! Well, even as I write, Roselyn and her husband, Eric Winter, are working to make Debbie's life a movie. Debbie's dreams were cut short, but we will make sure she's never forgotten. She was a dancer, an amazing performer who wanted to become famous, and she will. People will know about her, about the amazing girl who had the guts to follow her dream, to believe in love, to search for her happiness, and who, unfortunately, died searching for her dreams. If I had to guess, I would say Debbie wouldn't change anything from her life, as she was a woman who lived life to the fullest. To this day, I talk about Debbie as though I had met her in person. I speak with Celeste often. The telephone line still makes a strong connection.

This was a story I followed up on for years. Even after the trial started to get postponed time after frustrating time, and the media kind of forgot what had happened, I always kept in contact with Celeste, her sister, an amazing and brave woman, who appreciates every sign of affection and responds to every message about Debbie.

It was a year and a half after Debora's murder when I found out Fox International Channels and RCN (a Colombian network) were planning on launching a new Spanish network in Los Angeles, so I sent in my résumé.

I feel as if God is always sending me angels and puts them in my path. When I say angels, I mean people who somehow help you, trust you without knowing you, or give you a hand. This particular angel is Rolando Nichols, who is now the main news anchor for our network. He trusted me without knowing too much about me. Thanks to him I was given the opportunity to come live in Los Angeles and work for what is now called MundoFox national network. It was an unforgettable experience to be part of the launching of a new network, and to make history, at least in the Spanish-speaking world in the United States. It happened on August 13, 2012.

Now at MundoFox, my work has been awarded three Gabriel Awards, sponsored by the Catholic Academy of Communication Professionals for Excellence in Journalism, for two consecutive years for the best coverage of the Virgen de Guadalupe. The most recent one was for the Best Public Affairs series, a story of a woman who unfortunately ended up dying of cancer, but for whom we at the network launched a campaign to help her raise the money she needed for the hospital bills, for her family and for a treatment she never got to try.

As I said, Debora's trial kept on being postponed. Every time we thought it could happen, Diana, myself, and Celeste, I would request vacation time to go to Las Vegas and had to end up canceling many times because the trial was off again. It finally did happen, and even though I could not go to Vegas, our local MundoFox station covered it as well as all the other media outlets.

It was a long wait before I was able to write the words Debbie and her family were waiting for, for almost four years: "Justice has been served." Nevertheless, I know everything happens for a reason: the wait, the people I met during this journey, and what I got from it, as a human being, is priceless. On a personal level, I now strongly believe Debora wanted me to know more about her life so I could learn from her mistakes. Just like a good friend of mine always tells me, "Let go and let God." Debbie never let go of her love for Jason. It's hard to do it, but we should all walk out of any circumstance that's causing us harm, and even pain. Deep in our hearts, we have the answer.

Debbie, Diana, Roselyn, thank you for coming into my life.

ACKNOWLEDGMENTS

Thank you, Diego Arias, for serving as intermediary between the two of us.

A special thanks to Rene Delgadillo, Sonya Sonnenberg, and Merriliz Monzon, loyal friends of Debbie's who were always available and willing to speak on her behalf.

We thank former Las Vegas Metropolitan Police Department public information officer Jacinto Rivera; news director Adriana Areal; news producers Wilma Roman Abreu, Marisa Venegas, and Jeannette Casal-Miranda; and Dr. Luis Gaviria. Also, a special thanks to news producer Jairo Marín.

Also, thanks to all of those involved in Debbie's life, like Mia Guerrero, Matthew Guerrero, and Lorenzo Buitrón.

And thanks to Rebeca Ferreira and Annette Scott for your activism, and Olga Hervis for your expertise.

To Celeste Flores-Narvaez, kudos for your eternal

loyalty to your sister, your patience, and your forbearance. Above all, for your passion.

The attorneys were both wonderful. Abel Yáñez, the defense attorney, who was candid and objective, and the stellar and dynamic prosecutor, Marc DiGiacomo. Prosecutor Michelle Fleck, so kind, and also stellar and always articulate. And attorney Luke Ciciliano, personal friend of Debbie's who represented her once, and here made his presence felt again.

To psychic Gale St. John, thanks for bringing up the name of a "Rosalind" or "Rosalie" who would be involved in this project, which led us to pursue Roselyn Sanchez via Martha Melendez, so thank you Martha. And thanks to another Marta, Marta Sosa, for having us on her radio show to speak with Gale.

To the amazing, talented, and beautiful Roselyn Sanchez, thank you for identifying so strongly with Debbie. You will channel her beautifully and make everyone, as you said, "fall in love with her."

A very special shout-out to super-agent Linda Langton, who is "absolutely fabulous!"

—Diana Montané and Carolina Sarassa